THE MODERN PRESIDENCY

second edition

THE MODERN PRESIDENCY

second edition

Grant McConnell

St. Martin's Press
New York

Library of Congress Catalog Card Number: 73-91473

Copyright © 1976 by St. Martin's Press, Inc.

All Rights Reserved.

Manufactured in the United States of America.

09876
fedcb

For information, write: St. Martin's Press, Inc.,
175 Fifth Avenue, New York, N. Y.   10010

Preface

T he presidency of the United States is the embodiment of some of the most striking ironies of the modern era. The apex of a government instituted to replace rule by a monarchy, it has been termed an elective kingship and its setting likened to a court. Designed to function as one element of a carefully calculated plan of checks and balances, it is ambiguous in its definition and uncertain in its boundaries. Praised and feared for its promise of great power, it recurrently betrays something amounting to impotence. Subject to changing shape and character by the personalities of individuals who occupy it, it is increasingly institutionalized.

Much of the fascination the office holds for Americans, and for others as well, consists in its very elusiveness. But this elusiveness is not the sort that derives from remoteness or secrecy; indeed, there is, if anything, a surfeit of information about the office and the activities of its holder. Rather, it is the consequence of the complexities and kaleidoscopic changes that are characteristic of American institutions and American society in general, for in ways not always foreseen or intended the presidency reflects the nation and its people. It is, moreover, intricately meshed with the other institutions of government. To abstract it from them for separate examination is to tear the web and to perceive but shreds of the reality.

The study of the presidency, then, is hardly less than the study of American government and politics. And yet it is not possible to see such a whole with one glance, however sweeping or penetrating. At best there is the hope that, in examining a single part, an awareness of those other parts and their interrelatedness may be conveyed. This book was written with such a hope. Its picture of the presidency is intended to be one facet of a political whole and not something separate and apart. Inevitably, with the passage of time, changes occur in both the whole and the parts. Some of these are tidal in nature and were there to be seen before. Others are more dramatic and more obvious. Both kinds of change can be important, but there is a danger that the dramatic flow of day-to-day events may be taken as having an untrue significance. Certainly the era of the late 1960s and the early 1970s was a time of national stress that afflicted the presidency as much as any institution. But are we far enough removed from these events to judge their real significance? This book, originally written in a time of waning optimism, has been revised in a time of pessimism, and so there is a chance it may reflect too much the latter mood. The attempt has nevertheless been made to avoid this extreme, an attempt bolstered by the conviction that, whatever the changes of recent years have been, the continuities are more important.

G. M.

Contents

THE MODERN PRESIDENCY

second edition

Myth and Symbol

chapter one

*T*he American presidency is the most conspicuous office in the world. By reputation also the most powerful office, it sooner or later becomes a focus of every important crisis that afflicts the peoples of the earth. Its own crises are those of the American republic itself; they often send reverberations across the seas. How it is conducted affects the fates of nations and can tip the scales of life and death for millions.

It is inevitable that an office of such majesty should draw a degree of attention overshadowing that given Congress, the Supreme Court, the states, and all the other institutions of the nation—an attention that is frequently fearful yet also often bordering on worship. Thirty minutes after President John F. Kennedy was shot in 1963, two out of three adult Americans knew of the event; within another hour nine out of ten knew. His funeral was hardly over before the making of a myth began; the death of Lincoln was the parallel that leapt to every mind. When Franklin D. Roosevelt died in 1945, the nation was shaken as it had been by only a very few other events of his turbulent era. Abraham Lincoln and Franklin Roosevelt were both wartime presidents and among the great figures of history, and so there may be nothing astonishing about the great outpouring of grief that marked these moments. And yet, similar waves of emotion appeared with the deaths of William McKinley and Warren G. Harding, neither of whom was a crisis president or a chief executive of heroic stature. Even the long drawn-out drama of the unseating of Richard M. Nixon was touched with an almost epic quality despite the sordid character of the acts for which he was brought down.

For better or worse, the presidency is intimately linked to the entire web of government in the United States. Certainly the work of government will go on if there is a lapse at its top. Routines will be carried out in their normal manner, and decisions of some consequence will be made. Moreover, even a president who seeks to change the course of things as they have been will find the undertaking difficult. The government is an awkward and cumbersome machine, captive to its own momentum and without visible controls. Nevertheless, it remains true that, without the presidency or without a president of at least minimal adequacy, the entire system would be very different in a multitude of ways, not all of which could be foreseen.

Recurrently in American history, a latent fear of the presidency has risen to the surface, a fear that it would be transformed into a tyrant's throne. National independence came only after a war in which the personification of the enemy was the English king; the Declaration of Independence contained as justification for the drastic act of rebellion a long list of grievances against that king. The Americans were not going to substitute a native tyrant for the one they had just cast off. And during the long debate over formulation and adoption of the Constitution, there were repeated expressions of fears that the office of president it created would turn out to be a monarchy. Quite probably, the prospect of the known quantity of George Washington as the nearly certain first president was the factor that saved the Constitution from being rejected on this score alone. The fear emerged again in the time of Andrew Jackson; he was caricatured, not entirely facetiously, as "King Andrew." Abraham Lincoln again stirred the fear; certainly his actions, however necessary they might have been in the face of the greatest crisis the nation has known, did not stop at the bounds set by the Constitution.

As the power of the United States in world affairs has grown, the fear of the presidency has spread overseas. Europeans, perhaps reflecting their reduced status in the world after World War II, have expressed dismay over the ability of an American leader to take actions profoundly affecting their interests and security after only a perfunctory consultation with their own governments. In this light it was easy to imagine that some future president might act with ruthless disregard for the well-being of lesser nations. Certainly the picture of Franklin Roosevelt conferring with Stalin and presuming to settle the shape of the world during 1944-1945, while giving the leaders of Britain, France, and China only minor roles, was ominous. So perhaps it was not surprising to hear a Frenchman, Amaury de Riencourt, declare, "We must see in the President of the United States not merely the Chief Executive of one of the Western democracies, but one already endowed with powers of truly Caesarian magnitude." Just a few years after this statement was made, there was a venture in Caesarism at Cuba's Bay of Pigs. It was an abject failure, but perhaps it provided evidence that the theory of the coming of American Caesars was correct, if premature. And, indeed, better evidence was on the way.

Americans have always been doubtful and divided on matters of foreign policy and anything to do with other peoples. On the one hand, they have been willing to indulge a fierce national pride to the extent of supporting strong retaliation for foreign insults; on the other hand, they have frequently sought to withdraw from dealings with the peoples of less enlightened places. And they have been equally willing to go to massive war and to launch the most ambitious crusades for peace the world has known. Inevitably, these contradictory and often passionate pressures have converged on the president as the inescapable wielder of America's foreign and military powers. But for the American public, the significance of these powers has been more domestic than foreign: the launching of American expeditionary forces abroad has sooner or later aroused deep fear of domestic dictatorship. This fear has grown in substance since World War II. The Korean and Vietnam wars, as well as lesser military ventures in Cuba, the Dominican Republic, and Lebanon, have given evidence that a president can, within a matter of hours, unleash forces that may affect the liberties of millions of Americans.

When Lyndon B. Johnson used an ambiguous incident involving a few North Vietnamese gunboats and an American destroyer in the Tonkin Gulf to obtain a congressional assent for extended use of American force in Indochina, it seemed to many that he had circumvented the constitutional requirement of a declaration of war. Similarly, when Richard Nixon expanded a very real war into the territory of Cambodia, it was evident that the power to make war, with its attendant powers to conscript men and regulate industry, had become firmly lodged in the presidential office. After the fall of Richard Nixon, many Americans, including numerous members of Congress, swore that the presidency must be curbed in its war-making powers. And yet, within a matter of months, an unelected president ordered United States armed forces to attack those of a small country to obtain the release of an American freighter that had been detained—and received widespread public approval for his actions.

These events have been ominous indeed, particularly in view of the fact that all may have been substantive mistakes. The problem becomes more difficult, however, when the need for action seems more real and the success more apparent. When John Kennedy confronted the nuclear might of the Soviet Union and forced Premier Khrushchev to order the hasty withdrawal of the missiles installed in Cuba, the power of the presidency was as potent as in the incidents mentioned earlier. Nevertheless, the success of the presidential actions and the obviously deeper nature of the crisis seem in retrospect to have lent authority to those actions, just as the gravity of the Civil War crisis did to Lincoln's emancipation proclamation.

Whatever the fears regarding the presidency and whatever their basis in reality, in times of crisis the powers of the office are likely to be very great indeed. And these powers derive directly from the support of the American people. This is clearest in crises of war and foreign affairs; at such moments the president is the symbol of the nation, and the calls for unity are most heeded. The nation, seemingly the day before no more than an abstraction covering a horde of contesting factions, suddenly becomes a vivid reality, and its president, like its flag, becomes a rallying point for all Americans.

In domestic affairs, however, the magic is far weaker. Lincoln was able to exercise dictatorial powers only because the crisis was one of war. In the 1930s Franklin Roosevelt was able for a short few months to get Congress to abandon its normal rituals and give him powers held by no predecessor, but even the depth of the economic crisis could not sustain his exercise of those powers for long. Great disputes soon broke out, and most of them quickly involved the president himself. There were available no devices of coercion or suppression of opponents, even had he been willing to use them. And when Richard Nixon sought to use the intelligence and police forces of the national establishment against his "enemies," the reaction was strong and effective; he found that he had destroyed the very myth of national embodiment on which the effectiveness of his office depended.

The power and character of the presidency have never been fixed on certain elements of American government. Both have fluctuated with the times and with the men who have held the office. Woodrow Wilson, before he became president, remarked, "The President is at liberty and conscience to be as big a man as he can." Wilson discovered when he held the office, however, that there were limits other than those of law and conscience to what he could do. These were limits set by the unwillingness of the American people to accept his projects. It was ultimately a limitation of this sort, rather than a matter of law, that brought Nixon's presidency to an end.

Although the presidency is a very real office with space, desks, and staff, it is ultimately elusive and almost insubstantial. This is a great paradox, given the reputation and power of the presidency. For, just as it is impossible ever to know precisely how far a president may go in his actions, it is difficult to say what his power consists of or whence it comes. This sometimes leads to confusion between substance and manner—or "style," as it was fashionable to term it in the Kennedy era. President Kennedy's manner was forceful and masterful. His office, and indeed the entire executive branch of government, gave the appearance of unity and furious activity. Theodore Roosevelt had an even more vigorous manner and, through his well-publicized adventures in the Wild West and on San Juan Hill, established a reputation of activism that frightened many. By some tests, however, the immediate successors of these two presidents, Lyndon Johnson and William Howard Taft, respectively, had better claims to accomplishment. Johnson was vastly more successful in completing legislation than Kennedy, and Taft was a much stronger foe of the trusts than Roosevelt. While the appearance of power is sometimes mistaken for the substance of power, appearance can occasionally be a useful substitute for reality and indeed may even become reality. For the most part, however, style is a deceptive index of actual power.

At the moment of American independence, executive power was the form of power most feared and hated by the rebelling colonists. The longest part of the Declaration of Independence was a list of grievances against the king. Yet, within little more than a decade the ex-revolutionaries had established a strong executive power, which in time was to call forth the judgment of Henry Jones Ford that here was a revival of "the oldest political institution of the race, the elective kingship."

Experience under the Articles of Confederation was disillusioning to the few but intellectually distinguished and influential men who took it upon themselves to frame a new instrument of government. The Revolution had been fought without any genuine executive, indeed without any genuine central government other than Congress, which was itself little more than an assembly of ambassadors from the states. The war had often gone poorly as these ambassadors failed to persuade their sovereigns to meet the financial and other obligations they had undertaken. The army sometimes went unpaid, and occasionally the troops melted away under the eyes of their supposed commanders. But the war had been won, and perhaps it was reasonable to suppose that such a haphazard arrangement would do for the less rigorous conditions of peace. As each subsequent war has done, however, the revolutionary war provided a definition of goals and a discipline that disappeared with peace. In some ways peace was a sterner test of government. The impulse to unity and cooperation was gone, and the absence of an institution capable of governing the new nation was alarming.

Though federalism and the separation of powers are distinct principles in the American political system, the two were related to a common problem—how to achieve a minimal unity among the factions that made up the bravely announced union. Some of the most powerful factions adhered to the preexisting units of the states. To alter the central state's power was to change factional power; yet a nation could not be created without attaching power-holders to it rather than to the separate states. Federalism was the particular compromise by which this seemingly impossible problem was partially solved. At the same time, an institutionalization of the union effected among the states and the many factions was imperative. Congress could not serve in this manner, for its vices were precisely those in need of moderation. The presidency was the means chosen, and its deliberate counterbalancing in the separation of powers was the compromise by which the political union became possible.

Among the many decisions reached by the men who met in Philadelphia in 1787, none was more fateful than the formulation of the presidency as a single executive chosen independently of the legislature. A plural executive chosen by Congress, as urged in the New Jersey plan, would have made the adoption of the new Constitution easier and more certain. It would have greatly mitigated the conflict between executive and legislature that has vexed so much of American history. It would not, however, have erased the underlying problem confronting the building of a nation; it would instead have tipped the scales toward division and disunion. Such an executive could hardly have avoided representing the centrifugal tendencies that have persisted throughout the years of American nationhood.

The decision, finally, for a single executive appears in the Constitution simply and directly: Article II states, "The executive power shall be vested in a President of the United States of America." It does not provide for a share in this power by the vice-president nor for a council attached to the president's office (an idea advanced in various forms at Philadelphia to diminish the monarchic aspect of the office). A primary quality of the executive, as Hamilton argued forcefully in *The Federalist,* must be unity. At the same time, a compromise has been provided, not only in the formal separation of powers but also in the many checks and balances scattered through the document.

On the issue of the presidency, it is difficult to escape a sense that the framers of the Constitution took considerable pride in their handiwork. They had solved a very difficult problem in practical politics and had, moreover, founded their solution on what was, in their eyes, the most solid kind of political theory. The practical compromise itself embodied the ideal of balanced government, which the best thinking of the time admired.

Considering the care and skill that shaped the Constitution as a whole and the provisions on the presidency in particular, however, Article II, the part devoted to the office, is astonishingly brief—almost, one feels, incomplete. The first section of this article is the longest and deals principally with the eligibility and choice of the president. It touches on his compensation and states the oath of office; it creates the vice-presidency but characteristically leaves much ambiguous about this office. Section 2 carries a list of presidential powers. The president shall be commander in chief of the armed forces. He may require the written opinions of the heads of unspecified executive departments; he may grant reprieves and pardons. He may, with the advice and consent of the Senate, make treaties; he may appoint ambassadors, public ministers, consuls, and judges of the Supreme Court, again by and with the advice and consent of the Senate; he may fill vacancies during Senate recesses. He is required to inform Congress of the state of the nation and recommend measures; he may convene both houses and adjourn them when they disagree on a time of adjournment; he must receive ambassadors and other public ministers; he must commission all officers of the United States; and he must take care that the laws be faithfully executed. The last section of the article provides for removal from office, upon impeachment and conviction, of the president, the vice-president, and all civil officers of the United States.

Whether taken as a mandate of power or as a description of the office, Article II and the few supplementary passages elsewhere in the Constitution are grossly inadequate. The list of functions and duties assigned the president is short and sketchy; at points, it is vague and trivial. To read it without reference to subsequent history is to discover more questions than answers. Just what process of treaty making is contemplated? What does appointments "by and with the advice and consent of the Senate" mean? Why should space be taken to empower the president to require the opinion in writing of the principal officer in each executive department? What are the executive departments? Are their principal officers otherwise directly responsible to Congress? Why should it be necessary to require the president to report to Congress on the state of the union? Does the oath of office confer any power on him that he would not otherwise have? What is implied by the statement that "he shall take care that the laws be faithfully executed"? This might appear to be a general mandate to manage the government, but it is only a fragment of a sentence and is so placed that it is capped by the specific requirement that he shall commission all the officers of the United States.

Neither in whole nor in part do the provisions on the presidency shed much light on the nature of the office. The items that are clear—the power to give pardons and reprieves, for example—are minor. What is significant—the opening sentence of Article II and the "take care that the laws be faithfully executed" clause—is cryptic. Even the meaning of the commander-in-chief clause is ambiguous. The relationship between president and Congress is implied rather than stated, and even the implication is understandable only in light of the well-known adherence of the framers to the doctrine of the separation of powers. The greater clarity of Article I on the powers of Congress suggests that the power of the president could come only from congressional enactment. And yet, if this were so, why should the few items of power given the president in Article II be stated at all? It is difficult to avoid the conclusion that either the framers were extraordinarily careless with this part of their work, or they were unaware of the implications of what they were creating. The former is too harsh a judgment; the latter is more probable.

The conditions of government, like those of life itself, in eighteenth-century America were vastly different from those the presidency has had to serve since. In a design intended to endure far into the future, as the Constitution was, freedom from rigidity was a virtue and vagueness easily tolerated. Only the most essential features could be specified, and, even with these, there could be no certainty that things would evolve as planned. The mark of the framers' success with the presidency was that the essentials were incorporated in the office, and they have endured: a single executive, chosen independently of Congress, whose power is limited. It would be impossible to point to any single passage that lays down this last and most important characteristic, but it was everywhere implicit and has persisted down to the present.

For the rest, the presidency is the work of the presidents. They have not been free to do with the office whatever they have wished or thought desirable for the nation. Congress has persistently taken a different view of the office from that taken by the presidents and has often been able to frustrate presidential plans and hopes. The Supreme Court on occasion has limited the office. The federal structure of the nation, as expressed in Congress and in other less obvious ways, has severely curtailed its possibilities. And the American people have set barriers to White House ambitions. Within all these limitations, however, the presidents have been able to create the presidency as we know it today, the most majestic political office of modern times.

The history of the presidency has been a continuing dialogue among the presidents over whether the office is endowed with some inner sources of power or not. This is the debate between holders of the "weak" and the "strong" conceptions of the office. Although the differences between these views have been great, they have never been polar: even the proponents of the "strong" position have recognized the existence of limits, and the "weak" presidents have sometimes acted without reference to specific authorization in the Constitution or in legislation.

The point that embodied perhaps the single essential characteristic of the office was made by George Washington: that the president could and must act at times on his own authority—and that there is such authority. Implicit throughout Washington's presidency, this view came out most clearly in foreign affairs, the area of policy where challenge was most difficult. When war recommenced between France and England in 1793, Washington was determined that America should remain apart from the conflict. The young government accordingly issued a proclamation of neutrality (although the word *neutrality* was not used in view of the divergent sympathies toward the combatants within Washington's cabinet). Controversy immediately broke out over the constitutional propriety of this step. Hamilton, supporting the presidential action, pointed to the opening statement of Article II, that the executive power is vested in the president, and to the "take care" clause. Though only a few specific powers were enumerated as the president's—treaty making, receiving ambassadors, and so on—no limitation to these alone was implied. Thus, the only limitations to presidential exercise of *executive power,* Hamilton held, were those expressed in the Constitution.

Hamilton's conclusion that the proclamation was within the president's power leaped past the question of whether the action was executive in nature. Madison, speaking for the opposition led by Jefferson, caught the gap in reasoning and denied the assumption that such action was executive. Hamilton and Washington nevertheless won the day. The real difficulty that the Madisonian argument encountered over time was that the distinction between executive and legislative power was less clear and definitive than Madison or Jefferson (or, indeed, Hamilton) assumed. Washington's act, following Hamilton's argument, helped establish the more basic principle that there were reserves of power in the presidency and that these must be used by the presidents. The formal constitutional argument was serious, but it was a reflection of the large dispute between two general visions of the presidency. The practice of Washington did much to reduce this dispute to one of definition of the boundaries of presidential power. From his time forward, whatever the formal arguments might be, the president was neither a figurehead nor an automaton applying legislative and constitutional prescriptions.

Jefferson's position was something of a paradox. He had opposed Washington's neutrality proclamation on the ground that it was not within executive power. When the presidency fell to Jefferson, then, it was reasonable to suppose that the office would become very different and more limited. John Marshall, however, made an acute prediction that, as Edward S. Corwin has pointed out, proved fundamentally correct: Jefferson would enhance his power as president but weaken the office. As a party manager, Jefferson demonstrated the possibility of manipulating Congress, particularly the House of Representatives. Relying on this basis of power, he was able to act vigorously, but his personal talent was not readily deeded to his successors. Both Madison and Monroe accordingly yielded up to Congress much of what the presidency had meant so far.

This lapse in the character of the office ended abruptly with the election of Andrew Jackson. There is an almost inescapable tendency to read history retrospectively, and for this reason the popular nature of Jackson's administration has sometimes been exaggerated. A broadening of the suffrage had been under way, but it was not as dramatic as it has sometimes seemed. Jackson's men, moreover, were not as different from their predecessors or so committed to the spoils system as they have sometimes been represented. Nevertheless, Jackson did understand popular appeals, and he made them. Here, probably, was his particular gift to the office: he demonstrated what was inherent in the presidency but had been obscured in previous thinking about it—that the president is a popular figure. He is popular because he commands the attention and often the imagination of the multitude; as a result he has large and frequent opportunities to enhance his power. He is also popular in that, simply by virtue of the vast scope of his constituency, he is less beholden than Congress to particular fragments of the nation. The peculiar history of the American struggle for independence had marked monarchy as unpopular; when the cry of monarchy was raised against Andrew Jackson by Clay, Webster, and others, however, its lack of force was apparent.

Jackson is variously said to have restored the presidency, to have remade it, and to have been the first real president. He has been acclaimed as the first incumbent of the office who stood for the interests and desires of the mass of the people. The issues of his time, however, were different from those that have since invoked class interpretations and in which presidents have stood as popular figures. The Jacksonian era was turbulent, and the disputes still raging about its conflicts are probably too easily seen in sharper terms than the muddied issues of his time justify. Certainly there is a striking paradox about Jackson himself: he favored states' rights but insisted on the autonomy of his own power as president against the pretensions of Congress, the focus of divisiveness. He was willing to recognize congressional power to interpret the Constitution but insisted on his own power as president to interpret the document and to act on that interpretation. The outcome, as with his determined assault that culminated in the destruction of the Bank of the United States, was the establishment of the presidential capacity for *action*. His effective insistence that the members of his administration were responsible to him and not directly to Congress was as important as his sheer activism. This issue of the path of responsibility of administration members was not settled by Jackson—it is still alive today—but Jackson's fire and fury did more than anything else to influence the trend of things.

The role Lincoln played and the measure of his impact on the presidency pose difficult problems in assessing the office. More than any president after Washington, he assumed the role of national leader. More than any president before or after, he brushed aside the limitations supposedly inherent in the office.

The statements that he was a dictator miss the mark, but his actions at several points clearly crossed the bounds of legality. He has had no imitators in these actions, and it is unlikely that there will be any. Yet his influence on the presidency has to be accounted one of the most important in the entire history of the office.

His specific contribution in constitutional terms was to invoke the "commander-in-chief" clause and create from it the "war power" of the president. It is hard to believe that the framers had any inkling when they endorsed the clause that it would be used as Lincoln used it. It is equally unthinkable, of course, that they could have imagined the ramifications of modern war, of which the Civil War was the prototype. The "war power," however, has remained vague and ill-defined down to the present. Although it has been invoked in both world wars, its users have been uneasy about it and have sought to bolster it with references to legislation. Indeed, Lincoln seems at first to have relied almost casually upon Congress to ratify his actions after the fact, as for example in his wartime advance of public funds without apparent congressional authority.

Despite his virtual creation of this ambiguous, and probably dangerous, constitutional doctrine, Lincoln's importance lay in the intangible and elusive central quality he brought to the office, leadership. Lincoln was a poor administrator, despite his choice of able cabinet members. He sometimes seemed hesitant and self-doubting; he was bitterly hated in his time. He is the one president against whom the charge of dictator has any substance. Yet of all the presidents, he was the greatest national defender of the Constitution. His legacy is an office that in crisis rises as the embodiment of the nation and a tragedy-touched myth that will color the presidency as long as the office endures.

As it did after Jackson and after Jefferson, the presidency contracted after Lincoln. The crisis past and Lincoln gone, Congress reasserted itself. Distinguished students of public affairs came to hold the presidency in such low esteem that a foreigner, Lord Bryce, discussed the proposition "Why great men are not chosen Presidents." A brilliant young American scholar named Woodrow Wilson titled his examination of the American system *Congressional Government,* indicating his strongly stated thesis. This book, Wilson's first, was written very near the presidency's nadir, at a time of cynicism toward public affairs. But the very changes that made government and the presidency almost insignificant in time produced their own reaction. Farmers' and workingmen's movements signaled the discontent beneath the surface. Gradually the public temper changed, and a movement for reform took shape.

Concurrently, the renewal of the office came about, though gradually and through the work of no single president. Theodore Roosevelt's flamboyant style once more placed the presidency in center stage, and the reascendance began. Princeton's Woodrow Wilson rather belatedly reassessed the presidency and in 1907 deplored that some presidents, "more theorists than statesmen," had failed to use the full power they might legitimately have used. He concluded that the presidency "is the vital place of action in the system." It is not altogether clear whether this good academic's dislike of theorists applied to the president then in office. Certainly Theodore Roosevelt had a definite view of the presidency, and he was explicit about it. Some years after leaving the office, Roosevelt stated in his *Autobiography* that as president he had insisted on "the theory that the executive power was limited only by specific restrictions and prohibitions appearing in the Constitution or imposed by the Congress under its constitutional powers. My view was that every executive officer, and above all every executive officer in high position, was a steward of the people bound actively and affirmatively to do all he could for the people. . . . I declined to adopt the view that what was imperatively necessary for the Nation could not be done by the President unless he could find some specific authorization to do it. My belief was that it was not only his right but his duty to do anything that the needs of the Nation demanded unless such action was forbidden by the Constitution or by the laws."

This categorical, and theoretical, assertion was denied a few years later by Roosevelt's successor, William Howard Taft. He wrote in *Our Chief Magistrate* that "the true view of the Executive function is, as I conceive it, that the President can exercise no power which cannot be fairly and reasonably traced to some specific grant of power or justly implied and included within such express grant as proper and necessary to its exercise. Such specific grant must be either in the Federal Constitution or in an act of Congress passed in pursuance thereof. There is no undefined residuum of power which he can exercise because it seems to him to be in the public interest."

The dispute was highly academic, however, since at the time each theorist wrote he was out of office. It fell to the ex-professor, Woodrow Wilson, to demonstrate the kind of presidency about which he had written. It was most certainly a strong one; its strength, however, derived largely from the war that prevailed through most of his term in office. When the United States entered the hostilities, the "war power" discovered by Lincoln served as a mantle for much of the industrial mobilization without which the war could not have been won. In this sense, the presidency was a source of legitimacy to the war effort. It could hardly have been otherwise with such vast and novel government activities. Ironically, however, Wilson discovered the boundaries of presidential power in the area in which it would have seemed to be most extensive—foreign relations. His ultimate failure was in the collapse of his designs for peace and the League of Nations.

With the defeat and death of Wilson, the presidency once more lapsed into the near desuetude that had overtaken it after the departure of the strong presidents of the past. Herbert Hoover might have become a strong president, after the manner of Lincoln or Jackson, but he was restrained by traits of personality, diffidence perhaps, and a commitment to methods that gave vetoes to every group that had reason to oppose specific actions. This commitment dated, curiously, from his experience as an administrator in Wilson's time.

The modern model of a strong president has been Franklin D. Roosevelt. Few presidents have been so denounced for the vigorous exercise of presidential power as he. His opponents claimed that he arrogated entirely new sources of power; even some of his supporters believed that this was true. In actuality, however, Roosevelt did no more than follow the examples of his predecessors, and he did not resort to the extremes that Lincoln had reached. Most of his program rested on congressional authorization, and where he acted without it, he relied upon his undoubted authority in foreign affairs. He cited the "war power," but for the most part he buttressed it by congressional authority as well. Less formally, Roosevelt relied upon the resources of party politics, an area in which he had incomparable skill. However, he also discovered in the trade associations and other groups so heavily deferred to by Hoover a source of support that Hoover had probably never envisaged. Moreover, Roosevelt had a tool hitherto unavailable or unexploited—the radio. The important thing, nevertheless, was that Roosevelt perceived his role as leader in a way that probably only two previous presidents—Lincoln and Jackson—had viewed the office.

The successors of Franklin Roosevelt have all been influenced by him—as much in power and style as in issues and policy. Harry S Truman came out of the Senate and might have been expected to hold a more exalted view of Congress than his predecessor. The vision of the presidency as it came from FDR persisted, however, and in his initiative with the Marshall Plan to assist in the economic recovery of war-torn Europe and his dismissal of General MacArthur after that general's insubordination, Truman demonstrated that he had a firm understanding of the realities of power in the presidency.

President Eisenhower represented the reaction to Franklin Roosevelt and, to a lesser degree, Truman; in this, Eisenhower was as much a captive of the Roosevelt myth as the others. He affirmed a view of the office as limited as Taft's; at times he seemed to believe that the American system of government simply required Congress to make the decisions and the president to carry them out. At critical moments, however, his actions belied his statements. In foreign affairs, as in his decision not to intervene in Indochina, and in domestic affairs, as in the civil rights struggle at Little Rock, Arkansas, he demonstrated that the presidency could not remain neutral. Neither John Kennedy nor Lyndon Johnson exhibited any doubt as to the nature of the presidency; in their hands it was unambiguously a position of leadership to be used to the fullest extent. Though each followed Franklin Roosevelt's example in relying heavily on congressional approval, both agreed that the initiative in the American system lies with the president. However much the proper means eluded him, Richard Nixon sought to be strong as a president, and Gerald R. Ford indicated that he too had no wish to be thought weak. Perhaps these are signs that the old Republican model of the presidency is now obsolete.

Yet, it may be premature to say that the curiously recurrent cycle of "strong" presidents followed by "weak" presidents has run its course and that henceforth the office will always be strong.

The administration of Eisenhower is not long past, and, measured by modern standards, it was weak. Moreover, in domestic affairs no president since Lincoln has attempted to circumvent Congress in his search for authority; the differences in modern presidents have consisted in their determination and capacity to cajole, manipulate, and coerce the legislators. Many important matters have moved beyond the consistent and effective scrutiny of Congress, but this is far more a product of the complexity of modern life than of any grasping by the chief executive; indeed, he has been afflicted by a similar problem. In foreign affairs there remains an open question as to whether the president's authority has grown or not.

Nevertheless, a large change in the character of the office has taken place. Strength and vigor are now the traits associated with its occupant and, probably, sought by the American people. These are the qualities most conspicuously appropriate for times of crisis. But in the modern era, crisis is seemingly chronic. Only for comparatively short periods since 1929 have there been opportunities to relax the sense of urgency that has been the modern lot; only in one of these, the Eisenhower era, has the nation indulged the theory of passive leadership in its highest office. Much has been said about "the imperial presidency" in recent years, and a strong mistrust of government has indeed developed. Despite a number of dram tic events centered in the highest office that induced one president to refrain from running for reelection and forced another to resign, it is notable that the standing of Congress in the esteem of the American people has fallen with that of the presidency.

Undoubtedly, relatively "weak" presidents will hold the office again. It is unlikely, however, that any will be as restrictive of view as Taft or as unassertive as Eisenhower. A new set of specifications has gradually evolved out of the years of crisis and the practice of modern presidents. These specifications can change again, but it will be difficult to make them require less strength than those that now prevail. It may, indeed, be that the strong-or-weak discrimination among presidents is no longer useful. A more elaborate scheme for characterizing presidents has been offered by James David Barber. In this scheme presidents are measured on two dimensions—whether they are active or passive and whether they are positive or negative. Barber finds that those who have been active and positive in outlook have been the most successful. Perhaps these dimensions constitute fuller criteria for judgment.

What Harold Laski said of the presidency a generation ago is even truer today: it is "the keystone of the American political arch." Yet the office remains almost impossible to define in any but the most superficial terms. Its powers can almost never be stated with certainty or precision. Their description in the Constitution is vague, disorganized, and misleading. They have expanded, and they have contracted. They have been interpreted in ways so radically different as to seem to refer to different offices. It would almost appear that the presidency is an open mandate for anything its occupant might choose to do with it; and foreign observers have variously predicted doom from it and copied it as a means of imposing tyrannies in their own lands.

But the dangers of the presidency have rarely derived from an excess of power in the office; they have often come from the uncertainty associated with it, sometimes from its patent inadequacy. It is likely that one of the major impulsions for Richard Nixon's attempts to retaliate against his political opponents was fear that he might fail in the conduct of the office if he relied only upon its proper resources. An elemental fact of the American presidency is that its powers are limited. The limits change with circumstances and are seldom precisely knowable in advance; they are no less real, however. To some degree they derive from the requirement of legislative authority for presidential action in most areas of policy.

The different constituencies of presidents and congressmen and the array of checks and balances insure differences between the two branches. Yet these mechanical checks by themselves do not necessarily limit presidential power. A president lucky in congressional elections and as skilled in the labyrinthine ways of legislative manipulation as Lyndon Johnson can do much to circumvent such checks. Increasingly, moreover, a great part of the work of government is "administrative" in nature and so complex that it is beyond much more than sporadic check by any elected representative of the people. The real limits on the power of the president come from the whole ethos of American government. The "mandate" given by election to the office is invariably ambiguous, and a president who relies on it to take drastic or wholly novel action is quickly in trouble. When there is deep national division on a major issue—the Vietnam War is a clear example—excessive presidential action leads to disaster, disaster shared by both president and nation.

The fundamental problem confronting both a president and American government as a whole is how to generate sufficient support for presidential action to match the needs of the nation. To do this, a president must mobilize his own constituency—the entire nation. The nation, however, is always something of an abstraction, a diverse, inchoate multitude of individuals spread across a vast expanse of land. To mobilize them is to give shape, to organize, to create and re-create the nation. The process is inevitably touched with mystery. Yet here is the essential dimension of the presidency. The greatest presidents have all ranked high on this scale, whatever their skills as administrators or legislative managers. All have made themselves national symbols; in so doing, they have given substance and purpose to the nation itself.

The People's Choice

chapter two

*T*he president performs one of his most important services before he ever reaches office. This service consists very simply of campaigning. He shares this service with his opponent and, indeed, with all the would-be candidates who have been eliminated in the long tortuous process of national choice; for the process of *selecting* a president is sometimes as important a feature of the office as the emergence of a particular individual as president. The contest—and all the conferring, caucusing, bargaining, and scheming—is the indispensable means by which each four years the record of the past is reviewed and a new assessment of the state of the nation is made by the people. Here is the way in which old compromises are examined, and perhaps revised, and new ones made among the many elements of the population. It is the occasion upon which every citizen is called on to think of him or herself as an American.

The process serving these awesome functions in the United States is without counterpart anywhere else on earth. Indeed, whether these functions are equally served elsewhere is questionable. Yet the process is noisy, disorderly, contentious, and absurd. The gap between the indignity of the process and the grandeur of the end is enormous. Most foreign observers regard the system as vulgar and ridiculous; most Americans look upon it as a form of circus, too, but they cannot withdraw their attention from it. There is even disappointment when, as at the Republican convention of 1972, the show is dull. It is certain that the system was never intended to be as it exists, and it is inconceivable that it ever could have been planned.

This paradox is a direct product of the democracy served by the process. The garish vulgarity that persists throughout the electoral campaign reflects the participation of the great multitude of the American people in the political life of the nation. The noise, the contention, and the crudities might be avoided if the campaign involved only the genteel and the well-bred. The price, however, would be enormous. To exclude part of the American public would be contrary to the ethos of democracy, and the consequences, though impossible to predict, would be dangerous.

Whatever the deficiencies of style characterizing presidential elections and their attendant rituals, the impressive fact is that the process largely achieves its ends. When the tumult has reached its climax on election eve, the issues confronting the nation have been put to debate—if not always in the highest intellectual manner or by the candidates themselves, at least by the press and television. At this moment, most citizens have reflected about national policies and how their own lives have been affected. Whether by contact, computer, or osmosis, the candidates have acquired a sense of the country and of the mood of its people. Subtly or crudely, they have changed their appeals and their programs to reflect that mood to the best of their abilities.

Ostensibly, the objective is no more than to win a numerical majority of the votes cast on election day. More is involved, however. No election is ever a simple reflection of the preference of the people for one man (or one party) instead of another; it is a composite register of the desires, frustrations, and aspirations of millions of individuals on an almost limitless number of matters. Some of these topics are concrete, some are theoretical, and some are so deeply emotional that they are beyond rational discussion. A presidential election is also a measure of intensity, for not all those entitled to vote do so; those who feel most strongly on matters touched by politics are the most likely to appear at the polls. The election also reflects elements of power other than sheer numbers of voters, for money and organization play their part in the mobilization of votes. These may be imperfections by the democratic ideal; they are nevertheless elements of power in the daily life of the nation. Ignored, they may well prove sources of later disorder.

So it is that, in the great calm of election day, the vote is cast and a decision emerges. But it is far more than a decision; it is the summation of an incalculable multitude of decisions, all of them simplified and compressed into the choice between two candidates. Should not the outcome be violent? For a whole season the charges, the innuendoes, the promises, and the words have been compounding until the mass would seem to have become critical and explosion certain. In a few breathless hours, however, the tallies are made and the results known. But long before the results are official, the loser goes on television to face virtually the entire nation; with every bit of manliness he can summon, he does his last great service to the nation in accepting the outcome. And the people, including as a simple matter of course all those in opposition, take the result as settled for another four years.

It is a monumental achievement. The choice of leaders in many lands has all too often culminated in civic dissension, defection of the defeated, and disorder. Even many modern nations have yet to solve the problem of peaceful succession. An orderly change of leaders, moreover, is a rough indicator of success in the elementary function of politics, maintaining peace and order among the citizens. That the outcome of elections is taken for granted in the United States is a measure of American political success. On the one occasion of utter political failure, the Civil War, an election was the precipitating cause.

Accommodation, peace, and harmony are the minimum ends of politics, but they are rarely sufficient. Virtually every political society confronts problems for which governmental power is essential. A stalemate of political forces within the nation might produce domestic peace, but it would rarely allow the solution of these other problems. Herein lies a great dilemma of modern politics. The American political system has been rather less successful in providing its government with the capacity to deal with objective problems than it has in gaining the acquiescence of the people in the government and its leaders. Presidential elections, in turn, have been less to blame for this shortcoming than the manner of choosing Congress and the sheer diversity of the nation. Nevertheless, a president who has been through the experience of a bitter campaign and a close election is likely to be aware of the narrow limits within which he can safely act. Such experiences deeply affected the presidencies of John Kennedy and Richard Nixon and undoubtedly had much to do with the excessive zeal exhibited in the latter's campaign for a second term.

The problem of the power to govern was probably uppermost in the minds of the framers of the Constitution as they formulated their plan for selecting a president. The Constitution was intended to establish a government capable of action. Since the presidency was central to the new conception, the framers intended to insure that only a man of high standing and competence would reach the presidency. Their constitutional plan, however, deferred to the states and their legislatures and thereby related the nation's highest office directly to the principle of federalism—and not merely through the president's relationship with Congress. Election was to be indirect, through the electors chosen as each state legislature might direct. The legislatures found many ways to pick the wise men who should serve as electors, but for the most part during the brief period the system actually operated as planned, the electors were the legislators themselves. The highly elaborate system provided a dense filter for the impulses of democracy.

The original plan ran into difficulty early when in 1800 Jefferson and Burr emerged with tied votes; the states then passed the Twelfth Amendment requiring electors to indicate which of their choices was for president and which for vice-president. Already, however, the original conception was on its way to obsolescence. The electors were required by the Constitution to meet in their various states and were thus precluded from acting as a single deliberative body. More important, the franchise was rapidly expanding, and other forms of political participation were not to be denied the masses of the people. The party system took discretion out of the hands of the "electors," who became mere registrants of the popular choice. It was democratization in spite of the Constitution.

Many of the constitutional provisions on presidential elections have, nevertheless, remained in force and have had significant effects. A president is still required to be a natural born citizen, a resident, and at least thirty-five years old. The electoral ballots are counted by states and go as state units, the winner of even the narrowest majority in a state taking all that state's electoral votes. The possibility thus remains that electoral votes may decide an election contrary to the indication of a simple count of all the popular votes. There is even the chance of an elector voting against the wishes of the party on whose ticket he was chosen; this has happened, though not in critical situations. Potentially more troublesome is the provision that, if no candidate wins a majority of electoral votes, the decision is thrown to the House of Representatives. Minority factions have thus been tempted to run candidates independently of the Republican and Democratic parties in the hope of getting a chance to maneuver in the House of Representatives and so extract concessions otherwise unobtainable. Under these circumstances, it is possible that a president might accede to office with a serious minority in popular votes and in an atmosphere deeply clouded by suspicion.

Of all the constitutional provisions concerning presidential elections, the most important is the one that requires the president to receive a majority of the electoral votes. This requirement has been one of the strongest forces making for a two-party system, which, in turn, is the essential element of the electoral process as it has operated since the rise of parties first disrupted the finely laid plans of the framers of the Constitution. The parties have substituted an entirely different method that no one ever planned or even foresaw. The Constitutional Convention was marked by strong fear of the evils that mass participation in politics might bring, a fear seemingly justified by the disorders preceding the calling of the convention. As the rise of parties relegated the electoral college to insignificance, however, the parties themselves provided the organizing principle by which the not-to-be-denied masses could take part in politics in an orderly and meaningful way.

Clearly, the party system has not met the tests of statesman-like discussion and consistent wisdom sought by the rationalist bias of the framers; nevertheless, it has allowed both the broad participation and the scope for accommodation demanded by the pragmatism of the American people. The appearance of parties effected perhaps the largest single change in the constitutional scheme, replacing the question, "Who will govern most wisely?" with, "Who will govern most acceptably?" Though the second question may be less inspiring, in a democracy it is more urgent. However wise his substantive decisions, a president who failed to retain the support of the people would have failed completely.

The substitution of a seemingly meaner question and a lower style of politics for those originally planned for the nation has distressed many Americans. This ambivalence about the political order extends to all the activities of parties and politicians; the very word *politics* has come to refer to party politics only—and to be a term of reprobation. The catalogue of sins ascribed to the normal activities of parties is long: the parties engage in endless arguments; they have no principles; they are too much alike; their leaders engage in cynical bargaining; they are corrupt; and so on ad infinitum. These charges contain a considerable degree of truth: the parties *are* contentious; they are pragmatic and ready to criticize their opponents; their daily life is filled with bargaining; and occasionally there are signs of corruption.

Nevertheless, the distress and contempt are misplaced. Without the arguments and the adversary stance of parties, public issues would get far less discussion, and decisions on them would often be less acceptable to the American people. Moreover, similarities between the major parties indicate that each is seeking to win the support of a majority of the voters. An election is a competition between attempts to fashion a compromise on all the issues that concern the voters, one that will appeal to the greatest number of them. Although they sometimes differ, the compromises frequently are similar, indicating similar responses to the same problem. (Note, however, that to be similar is not the same as to be unprincipled.) Beyond this, the parties do evolve different solutions, and they do differ on some important matters. If the differences were as great as some of the cynics appear to wish, however, the nation would be in serious danger of open conflict, and the parties would have failed in their ultimate mission of adjusting differences and preserving the social union. The fate of the campaigns of Barry Goldwater and George McGovern suggests the risk involved in seeming to propose sharp changes in national policy.

The larger functions just mentioned are by-products of the process and are not the day-to-day conscious intent of the parties. The specific function of any party is to attempt to elect its candidates to office. To winnow the potential candidates, the parties must weigh a complex array of considerations. The platforms that emerge—the statements on issues and policy—are part of the large process of political compromise, but they are more immediately directed to the goal of winning office. When these platforms and policy statements are bland, temporizing, and even vague, it is probably because they deal with matters on which the electorate is itself divided.

Not all elections serve the large and grand functions indicated here, however. In some local elections, the candidates are obscure, and the issues of policy may be so little discussed that they are hidden entirely. Such elections are usually marked by an absence of both party competition and widespread participation. The candidates who thus show up on the ballot seem to arrive there mostly by chance, and the whole affair takes on the character of a lottery. Able men may reach office this way, but it is unlikely that they will, and the candidates who succeed do so without benefit of the debate and controversy that best indicate the temper of those who will be governed.

Presidential elections are never of this character. The importance and drama of the office make these elections major events and insure that they are always contested. These elections reinforce the drive for party organization and for competition between the parties. Their influence extends to elective contests for offices that in nonpresidential years receive little attention. Here lies a curious paradox. The American party system is organized along federal lines, as laid out by the constitutional order. It has accordingly become a cliché that the parties are more local than national. Yet the parties often show more vigor and substance nationally than they do locally. Part of the explanation is that American parties are weaker and less well organized than is generally assumed. In many areas of the country, they scarcely exist, and in some states—California and Wisconsin, for example—they are heavily inhibited by laws that seek to deny them significant roles. The contest over the presidency often provides what impulse there is for party organization and competition. Without the presidency as a major focus, the American party system would probably be vastly weaker than it is.

Between presidential election years, the national party organizations dwindle to almost nothing. Some continuing party organization persists in Congress, but a visit to the national headquarters of either major party reveals only a small establishment engaged in little activity and exhibiting no sense of urgency. Compared to any of the strong interest-group organizations, the party structures are insignificant in the so-called off years. In some localities, it is true, party organization continues active, particularly if other elections must be faced there. But public participation in local party organizations is minor and often not desired.

When a presidential election approaches, however, the national organization comes to life. It rents lavish office space, which is pervaded by a great bustle of activity. Locally, the party machines spring into similar activity, and their emissaries seek out segments of the public that they have not seen since the previous presidential election. Where there is no local party organization other than the nominal body consisting of a few office holders—and this is not uncommon—machinery is hurriedly improvised to reach all those individuals who collectively are sovereign but who otherwise are voiceless.

Improvised and defective as it is, this machinery must find a candidate and get him elected. The first task is at least as important as the second. At the outset, the individuals who would like to become president and have some kind of qualifications are numerous. Probably most, however, are unknown nationally. Without machinery for their exposure, the election would be little more than a lottery. The results might occasionally be good, but there is no reason why they should be. The parties provide both a rough set of rules and tests for candidates to pass. These tests have a greater rationality than is sometimes evident. Usually a candidate who hopes to succeed must have national standing and high party rank. There have been exceptions; certainly Warren Harding was not a national figure, and Dwight Eisenhower had no known party affiliation until just before he was nominated. Generally, though, to be an effective president, a candidate has needed personal prestige and party experience.

A serious candidate who hopes to meet the tests imposed by the parties is thus typically a governor of a major northern state or a prominent senator. Again, this rule has not invariably been followed—Wendell Willkie was a corporation executive, Eisenhower was a general—but the highest political honor is usually reserved by the politicians for politicians. This is not merely the selfishness of a particular guild; it is also insurance that the candidate commands the trust of great numbers of his country- men and knows the ways of the political order through which he must act. Of all the posts that most nearly approach the presi- dency in the substance of their responsibility, governor and senator are closest. Like the presidency, they demand sensitivity to the needs and aspirations of large numbers of citizens. While the work of a governor is exclusively domestic, a senator's involves foreign affairs, and if there is reason for the recent preference of the senatorial route to presidential candidacy, perhaps it lies here.

Even after the field of candidates has been reduced by these first rules of practical eligibility, the list will normally still be too long for anything but a meaningless melee and will require further winnowing. The conventions that meet to make the final choices have little time, and much elimination must occur before they meet. The manner in which this is done certainly meets no ideal test, but the job does get done. Some of the process is informal and private: for example, the meetings among politi- cians that evaluate potential candidates in the years between elections. But the most important part comes in the trial period of approximately nine months before the general elections. This is when the candidates try to make themselves known and their ambitions discreetly but clearly understood. During this period, they face up to the ordeal of the primaries—or find good reasons for not doing so.

A presidential primary is a strange sort of election. Its results cannot be binding on the delegates in the maneuvering at the national convention. The choice given the voters who take part in the primaries—usually a small part of the electorate—sometimes does not include all the most important candidates. At best, a presidential primary is a rough test of the popularity of certain candidates; and this function might be served more accurately by scientific sampling of voter opinion.

The primaries are nevertheless useful: they dramatize the choices that must be made. They serve at least part of the function for which they were intended by allowing candidates not favored by party leaders to prove themselves if they can. George McGov- ern won his 1972 nomination through the primaries, even though the party leadership did not support him. The primaries also provide an opportunity to assess the importance of certain issues.

Thus, John Kennedy demonstrated in the 1960 primaries, particularly in West Virginia, that being Catholic was not a practical disqualification of his candidacy. Without this evidence behind him, he might well have failed in the national convention. The primaries do have some merits, then, despite their partial nature and their costliness. Ultimately, they winnow the serious and promising candidates from the frivolous and hopeless ones. Their importance in the selection of candidates is likely to grow.

The states that do not hold primaries—a now rapidly declining number—choose delegates to the national conventions at state convention, a process involving primarily the professional politicians. In such situations, personal connections between aspiring candidates and local leaders are at a premium. Though there is something discriminatory about that, this aspect should not be exaggerated; it is part of the political profession to be in touch with leaders in different localities, and a competent candidate will send emissaries to those states where he is not already well known. The state conventions' incentive to select a winner minimizes the bias that may arise from purely personal friendships or antagonisms. There is probably less emotionalism and more coldly rational assessment of candidates in the state conventions than in the primaries. Because the rational test applied is whether a candidate is likely to win, the ends of democracy are probably as well, if not better, served by the conventions as by the primaries. The effect of the increasing use of primaries is mixed: it permits a degree of direct popular participation in candidate selection, but it weakens the parties and their ability to negotiate compromises.

All this is preliminary to the big shows, the national conventions, which are perhaps the strangest working political bodies in the Western world. Nowhere else has the art of organizing spontaneity been more highly developed, and yet spontaneity somehow actually survives. Rational thinking is the last virtue to be expected from the mob scenes that these conventions present; yet some clear thinking goes on. Though the noise is deafening, people manage to be heard. Many of the speeches are endless and banal, but some are terse and good. Little that occurs on the floor is to be taken at face value, but little is utterly without point either. A national convention at moments has the air of a nineteenth-century revivalist meeting; at times it is like a great sporting event; and occasionally it resembles a street riot.

To an observer it is a marvel that any sensible achievement emerges from the national conventions, much less that any rationality operates. Yet there is a kind of rationality, and invariably the delegates nominate candidates *acknowledged* as those between whom the nation must choose at a general election. Usually, though not always, a rough framing of a symbolic compromise among the many factions of the American people also results.

It is tempting to assume that the real work of the convention goes on behind the scenes and that the visible show is itself meaningless or the product of manipulation by backstage wire-pullers. In part, this picture is correct. There are innumerable hotel-room meetings, countless telephone calls, and much covert, prearranged signaling. Many of these communications, however, are less private than the participants seem to believe, and not infrequently the secrets are shared with millions who sit in fascination before their television sets. Some of the "secrets" are deliberately planted in order to be revealed, but to a very considerable degree the supposedly devious maneuverings are open to public scrutiny. Intensive television coverage has made secrecy extremely difficult to maintain; indeed, it sometimes seems that the nationwide audience is better informed than many of the delegates as to what is occurring. For the rest, some of the crucial events appear on the floor in full session, beyond any hope of concealment. In the conventions at which an incumbent president is a candidate for reelection, there is, of course, usually only the problem of simulating drama.

Some candidates arrive at a contested convention without elaborate personal organizations and have little more in mind than to be available in case of stalemate among the frontrunners. Their chances are poor—no dark horse has been successful in recent times—but given the magnificence of the prize, hope springs eternal. The most serious candidates come well equipped. Probably none in history have been as meticulously prepared as John Kennedy in 1960 and Barry Goldwater in 1964. The Kennedy organization used strategically placed telephones on the floor, runners to bring messages where only footwork would serve, and even walkie-talkies. The planning for both of these men was minute and effective, foreseeing contingencies and taking every precaution. How much these skills of modern organization accounted for is difficult to say, since each of these men was obviously in front before the conventions met.

The excitement of a convention often begins over the seating of challenged delegates. These contests may relate to purely internal state quarrels; they may also reflect fundamental issues that could split the party and endanger its hopes of success at the polls. The Democratic conventions have had more than their share of such contests in recent years, most connected with civil rights, and have attempted reform of their rules of delegate selection in order to bring new segments of the electorate into the party process; the reform has not made the Democratic path any easier. Although the Republicans have on the whole been spared this ordeal, they may not be better off for having escaped it. As in many other spheres of American life, contest and even conflict sometimes confer benefits. The opening struggles give signs as to which way the winds are blowing in the party. The signs become clearer when the permanent chairman is chosen. The chairman's post is not just an honorary one, for he can influence the outcome of events by his choice among the competing voices clamoring for recognition at critical moments.

With the convention organized, the nominating speeches begin. Some are fairly perfunctory—for favorite sons who have no hope of nomination but are deemed worthy of honor or who serve to hold their delegations for bargaining purposes or for some more devious plan. As the real candidates are put forward, an extraordinary ritual of nineteenth-century oratory rings forth. "The man who . . ." becomes an incantation repeated again and again as the description of the as-yet-unnamed paladin mounts with rolling intensity and fervor, until the suspense can be carried no longer. Then the orator shouts out the name of the hero he is nominating. With a great roar, the convention explodes in mock surprise and delight, a wild parade erupts into the aisles, and, while the band plays and delegates cheer and noisemakers resound, the proceedings are brought to a halt. The process is repeated for each of the principal candidates, and gradually it begins to lose some of its synthetic drama. Though connoisseurs find subtle differences in the length and apparent ardor of the various demonstrations, these cognoscenti are few, and there are signs that public taste for this sort of thing is waning.

With the balloting, things become serious. There are certain standard gambits, to a large extent geared to building a band-wagon movement or, better yet, a steamroller. The latter, which would produce a first-ballot decision, would obviously be more impressive. This, however, is not always possible. And so the art of holding back certain blocs of votes to cast into the cauldron at a psychological moment and spread dismay into hostile ranks comes into its own. This specialized skill, like other esoteric arts, probably is less important than its practitioners are likely to admit. Ultimately, the bandwagon appears and nothing can stop it. The laggards, recognizing its approach, make a headlong scramble not to be left behind, and suddenly the convention is declaring its unanimity for the party's candidate.

What remains is anticlimax, although by no means unimportant. The choice of the vice-presidential candidate is now generally recognized as a matter for the presidential nominee to handle. Nevertheless, that choice is severely limited. If the struggle for the presidential nomination has been lively and touched with bitterness, there is a very strong reason to heal the wounds to party unity by choosing one of the defeated aspirants. The aspirant chosen, however, must represent a different core of strength, geographical and otherwise, than the successful nominee. Moreover, thought must be given to the presidential qualifications of the man chosen. All these considerations force the test of personal compatibility between the two nominees into a secondary position. Certainly John Nance Garner was less than a soulmate for Franklin D. Roosevelt, and Lyndon B. Johnson was not an intimate to the Kennedy organization's inner councils. Both of these combinations symbolized a bridge across the deepest geographical split in the nation. In all the madness of a convention, then, there is rationality. It is the rationality shared by nearly all who take part, the logic of winning the coming election. The motivation is, without question, selfish; it does, nonetheless, serve the important public function of formulating a broad compromise for the voting public to accept or reject.

The campaign begins formally on Labor Day. From then until the election, the candidates drive themselves and are driven by their commitments and their managers—which, if nothing else, tests their capacities for physical survival. American campaigns last longer than electoral campaigns in Europe, and critics regularly call for shorter campaigns. The voters, they claim, are bored; the costs are excessive and the whole affair a pointless distraction from the serious matters of life and government. Perhaps the development of television campaigning and extensive press reporting have now permitted voters to form earlier impressions of the choices before them. Often, it is suggested, they have made up their minds long before election day. Yet this is not always true, for close elections would not necessarily yield the same results were they held a month earlier. Moreover, there is a partly justified general suspicion that the television medium is susceptible to its own kind of theatrical deception in that it favors political "performers" who film well but who may not necessarily be the candidates who would succeed best in office. Moreover, the analogy to most European elections is faulty. The American president represents the entire nation—directly. He is more than a party leader, and once elected, he becomes chief executive in his own right. Besides, the physical magnitude of the United States at least creates a presumption that a campaign here is a greater undertaking than one elsewhere.

The really important ground for hesitating to accept the idea of a shorter campaign, however, is that the campaign experience is an essential preparation for a prospective president. The office has no training ground as such, and it is difficult to conceive that any curriculum to prepare a person for the presidency could ever be developed. In campaigning, a candidate is not only making (or failing to make) an impact on the voters; he is also exposing himself to all the diversity of the nation, its concerns and moods. Travel about the land and contact with great numbers of Americans insure some exposure to these concerns and moods. The traditional campaign is not ideal, but an adequate substitute would be difficult to devise. Even where the candidate is an incumbent president, it is highly useful that he renew his contact with those he must lead and meet attacks of even the most captious sort.

The criticism that presidential elections are too expensive has most frequently derived from an unspoken premise that *any* money spent on politics is wasted. This view is part of an attitude that holds the work of politics to be unimportant and lacking in seriousness, an attitude that is sometimes irrationally combined with charges that the works of politicians are dangerously mistaken. In fact, those efforts are often of the greatest importance, involving as they do the prospects of prosperity or depression and peace or war. It is certainly wrong to suggest that only small amounts of money should be spent on selecting a national leader and calling upon Americans to think about their common affairs. Nonetheless, as the Watergate affair abundantly showed, a gross excess of campaign funds can lead to their gross abuse. The more persistent money problem in elections is how to prevent the providers of that money from establishing unfair degrees of influence over successful candidates. A solution to this problem is not in sight; certainly it does not lie in a simple denial of all but trifling amounts of money to the work of politics.

Presidential campaigns differ from one another as circumstances vary. A few persistent conditions nevertheless produce recurrent responses. First, when an incumbent president is running for reelection, as, on the whole, he must if he is eligible, the campaign tends to revolve about his record and his program. The incumbent has great advantages: he is inevitably better known, and he is able to blur the distinction between his role as chief executive of the nation and his role as party nominee. His opponent is somehow guilty of bad taste, if not worse, in some eyes for criticizing a national symbol. The incumbent president need do and say nothing to reap this advantage; it is sufficient that he quietly stress the importance of his tasks as national leader. This is highly frustrating to his opponent but must be accepted. The incumbent president can refuse, quite rightly, to participate in television debates and so avoid casting reflected fame upon his rival. Whether for these reasons or because of sheer tradition, incumbent presidents can usually look forward to reelection.

When neither candidate is an incumbent president, the advantages are less consistently on one side. The candidate whose party holds the presidency at the time of election may be able to cite the virtues of experience and intimacy with the problems of state, as Nixon did in 1960. This approach is available if the candidate has been a conspicuous member of the outgoing administration, but it is not a strong advantage. The candidate of the opposing party, on the other hand, can appeal to the accumulated hostilities generated by the party in power. As the American system has worked in the past, there is apparently a limit on the time that one party may control the presidency without making too many enemies. This limit undoubtedly was reached in 1952, for example.

Each of the two major American parties reflects conditions peculiar to itself. The most obvious is the long-term hold of the Democrats on "the solid South." Observers are now looking for the final dissolution of this historic accident. It may be said that the election of 1964 provided the break, yet the accompanying increase of black voting and the continuing hold of the Democratic party on black loyalty cast doubt on its ultimate significance. There are other areas where traditional loyalties go strongly to one party or the other: Vermont, for example, is a proverbially Republican state. These loyalties are very stubborn indeed; the political systems that develop in such states tend to perpetuate them. Nevertheless, it would be rash to say that they are beyond possible challenge.

Since the New Deal, there has been something of a class difference in the core groups to which the major parties appeal most strongly. On the whole, the Republicans retain the loyalties of business and the wealthier parts of the electorate, while the Democrats have the advantage with lower income groups and labor. It is easy to exaggerate this difference, which, though real, is not a polar factor. To say that the Republicans have the money while the Democrats have the voters is a gross overstatement. The Democrats also collect money, and the Republicans also win elections. There are genuine differences between the two parties— matters of policy, for example—but they are seldom in diametric opposition.

The really important fact is that, for whatever reasons, the Democrats have in recent times enjoyed a three-to-two lead over the Republicans in voter identification. Party identification is a significant factor in choosing a president, perhaps more so than the appeals of personality or issues. By this logic, the Democrats ought to win consistently; they do not, of course. People with large incomes and more education are more likely to vote than those with lower incomes and less education. Thus, one apparent disadvantage of the Republicans is to some degree counterbalanced.

The basic difference in voter identification bears importantly on the strategies that underlie the campaigns of the two parties. The Democrats normally have everything to gain by appealing to party loyalty. Though this approach can be combined with appeals to party principles, the emphasis is on the idea that the candidate is a *Democratic* candidate. Thus, the task of the Democrats is to get out the vote. If they succeed in marking their candidate as the *party* candidate and insure a large voter turnout, they can reasonably expect to win. In contrast, the Republicans gain more by insisting that the campaign is between candidates and that the voters ought to choose the best man without regard to party. Their problem is to detach a substantial number of Democrats from the Democratic nominee while holding on to their own party identifiers; the former is more difficult. When a national hero like General Eisenhower is available, the Republican problem is most easily solved.

The matters of principles and policy are difficult for both parties. Each must, after all, look to the formulation of a majority of those who actually come to the polls. Clear statements on policy sometimes lose more votes than they gain. The Republican experience in 1964, when Senator Goldwater was especially forceful on a number of issues, and the Democratic disaster following Senator McGovern's equal clarity in 1972, are unlikely to tempt either party to sharpen its positions on the issues.

When, at long last, the election actually occurs, what is settled is very simply which man is going to be president and which party is going to have general influence over ("control of" is too strong) the executive branch of the government. The concurrent congressional and other elections are also influenced by the presidential election. But for the rest, what has been settled? In one sense, very little—and in another, a great deal. The specific pledges made during the campaign that must be redeemed are usually few and generally not vastly important. General Eisenhower's promise during his campaign to go to the Far East is as good an example of a specific pledge as can be found. It was, however, but a gesture—a token of intent to end the Korean War. In everyone's eyes the general intent was what counted, and it depended on more than a president's trip. Sometimes a claim is made that a winning candidate, by virtue of his success, has a "mandate" for a specific action. It can never be said that the voters intended some specific act. Yet there is a general mandate to the president to carry on the leadership of the nation. He has the authority of his constitutional powers as president, and to claim a mandate in any other sense is irrelevant and often a confession of weakness.

The electoral system is in a state of change today. The most notable fact is that the parties are not in healthy condition. The advent of television has to a considerable degree supplanted older techniques of campaigning and has rendered secondary in urgency the bargaining and compromising that have been the major preoccupations of each party. The principal political arts of the now dominant medium seem to be the making of "images" and the casting of personalities for the stellar roles. Ironically, this effect is accentuated by a strong disenchantment with "politics," which seems to be popularly equated with parties. Watergate contributed incalculably to the present public distaste, despite the fact that the scandals were associated with a personal campaign organization outside the Republican party, the Committee to Re-elect the President, itself a challenger to the party system. It is premature to say that the parties are headed for extinction; each has survived previous obituaries. Nevertheless, their present state is reason for concern.

The most important question to be asked about the process of electing a president is how well it has actually served its major purposes. There have been moments in American history when the electoral system and its attendant parties have seriously failed. For instance, the goal of maintaining a fundamental unity in the nation was not met in the campaign and election that gave Abraham Lincoln the presidency. The issues then before the nation could not be resolved by any process of compromise and accommodation; indeed, perhaps they were such that compromise and accommodation should not have occurred. In the election of 1892 the established party system failed markedly to encompass the demands of a large and seriously aggrieved segment of the population, the farmers. A new party, the Populists, appeared and demonstrated the strength and intensity of the farmers' grievances so clearly that they had to be taken into account in the following campaign. Moreover, it is at least arguable that the system was deaf to the grievances of working people during the first part of this century. It is impossible to say how close the country came to domestic upheaval in the depths of the Great Depression. But certainly it was a time of disaffection, which registered in 1932, and the political process has never been blind in this way since.

Failures such as those in 1860, 1892, and the twentieth century are more important than the deficiencies of style that our electoral campaigns regularly exhibit. The process of picking a president is noisy, undignified, and often absurd. Purists may well wish for more graceful campaigning, and more incisive and intellectually elevated debates. Quite possibly, however, achieving these desirable conditions might rob the process of much of its vitality and leave the ultimate winner with no accurate sense of the temper of the American people. A presidential election is, above all, an articulation of the mood of the electorate. It is by no means an ideal device, but it would be difficult to contrive a more accurate and more meaningful one.

A presidential election and all the processes of which it is the quadrennial culmination are vital parts, probably the most vital parts, of the life of American democracy. The essential quality of that democracy is compromise—compromise among the myriad elements that make up a nation of continental expanse. This accommodation is a continuing matter, but the existing balance is brought under review every four years, and the differences are reduced to a choice between two candidates for the presidency. The ultimate test is that the outcome be accepted as valid by the American people. With one exception, which eventuated in the Civil War, this validation has been given. The president, his opponent, and their supporting parties are the essential means for posing this regular test and precipitating the review by which it is passed.

President and
Congress

chapter three

Much that is crucial to American political life revolves about the relationship between the president and the Congress. When the framers of the Constitution established these two entities as coordinate branches of the new government, they undoubtedly considered that they were merely giving explicit recognition to a fundamental principle of government: that these two branches reflected two inherently different functions. The intricately contrived system of checks and balances that they added set the stage for a recurrent drama in American history, the contest between the two departments.

Separation of powers, especially the legislative and the executive powers, is often cited as a basic principle of American government. Whatever the vision of the founders, in actuality this principle has proved secondary to federalism, which the founders themselves hammered out with great originality. The president and the Congress both represent the nation; together they provide the authentication of policy and the consent without which popular government, perhaps any government, could not exist in the United States. They work, however, in utterly different ways. Partly, they differ in their activities—legislating and administering; more important, they represent the nation in different ways.

The president represents the nation as a whole, while the Congress represents it as a collection of states and congressional districts. The separation of the powers of the executive and legislative branches is the embodiment of federalism. Inevitably, because of the different constituencies of the president and the various senators and congressmen, a president is often sharply at odds with the views and purposes of many members of Congress. It would be comforting to assume that the many different positions that congressmen and senators take add up to a position as nationally oriented and as public-spirited as the president's, yet often the two branches arrive at quite different positions. Which is correct? Which more surely represents the people of the United States? It is difficult to predict which will prove *wiser*. As to which is more public-spirited, the answer is also ambiguous. Insofar as both president and Congress respond to the wishes of the public (and they both do so more frequently than they are given credit for), it is hard to show that one branch is better than the other.

In the degree to which they prefer *national* interests, however, there is a significant distinction. Members of Congress represent different publics, different from each other's and from the president's. Their constituencies vary widely, some consisting largely of rural areas, some of large cities, some of working-class districts, some of states where mining is overwhelmingly important, and so on; the president's constituency consists of all the people. Because the smaller constituencies emphasize particular interests, the aggregate representation offered by Congress does not equal that of the presidency. The consequence is that there are consistently some differences between the policy positions of Congress and those of the president. On the whole, the president tends to emphasize national considerations and the interests of a great diversity of people more often than Congress does. This is not to say that his position will necessarily always be "better"; not only can he make errors, but national interests, the interests that are most widely shared, should not always be preferred to particular interests. It is firmly in the American tradition to protect minorities. Nevertheless, it is true that very large differences of outlook are built into the government.

Although the tension between president and Congress is a persistent characteristic of the American governmental system, the locus of power has oscillated significantly between the two. Perhaps the most striking shift came with the death of Lincoln. During the Civil War he acted independently of Congress, treating it with near contempt. Congress struck back during the war, but it was really effective only after Lincoln was gone from the scene. In a very short period, the leaders of Congress virtually seized power and subjected Lincoln's successor to the humiliation of impeachment proceedings. Congressional power became so firmly established that several decades later it was entirely appropriate for a young scholar, Woodrow Wilson, to characterize the American pattern in the title of his first book as "congressional government," government, that is, by the standing committees of the House of Representatives. Wilson later had to revise his estimate.

These changes were neither the first nor the last of the oscillations. Indeed, the first came with the adoption of the Constitution itself. The very creation of the presidency marked a recession from the mistrust of the executive that had resulted from the hatred of the English king. In view of the subsequent development of relations between the president and Congress, it is curious that much of the dislike of legislatures stemmed from a sense that they were too popular, too democratic an element in the pattern. Just as Jefferson began to make the presidency into something of a popular organ, however, Congress reasserted itself, and until Jackson's presidency there was, as one writer has put it, a period of "congressional sovereignty." Jackson broke this condition by sheer force of personality and his willingness to exercise party leadership. Thus, the presidency assumed the role of popular advocate that it has held ever since.

Before Lincoln assumed his nearly dictatorial powers, there was another strong renewal of congressional power vis-à-vis the presidency. Buchanan may have been weak in his personal qualifications, but the congressional opposition he met would have frustrated even a more able and determined president. Buchanan's problems in this regard undoubtedly reinforced Lincoln's disinclination to go to Congress for authority before acting.

On the whole, national crises have marked the periods of the greatest growth in presidential versus congressional power. This growth has been most apparent in times of war, but it also occurred during the Great Depression of the 1930s. Its occurrence is not mere coincidence, however, as the executive has the greater capacity for action and bears a continuing responsibility. Nevertheless, in the oscillation of the preponderance of power, several other factors are important. First, a period of congressional dominance creates problems that, because of popular demand, must be acted upon and in time must be solved. Such problems and such demands were building throughout the latter part of the nineteenth-century period of "congressional government." Thus, for example, the widespread distress on the farms got little effective attention from government at this time. Thus also, the attack upon monopolies was halfhearted and ineffectual. Such problems helped produce the activist mood of Theodore Roosevelt and provided the basis for the program of Woodrow Wilson.

There is also the striking fact that, as Wilfred Binkley has observed, there has been a consistent difference between the sorts of presidents that the two major parties have produced. To a remarkable degree, the Democratic presidents have been strong, and the Republican presidents, on the whole, have been weak. In part, the difference is the work of chance, Democratic presidents having come to office in times of crisis more often than Republican presidents. In greater part, however, the difference lies in a distinct preference of the Democratic party for strong presidents. However fashionable it may be to emphasize the similarities between the two parties, here is a major point of difference between them.

Though it is difficult to establish just what the systems of belief are that lie beneath this party difference, it is possible to point to the beliefs of particular presidents. Thus, Woodrow Wilson had a vision of an American system of government that would be similar to the British; and Britain, of course, has no separation of powers. Certainly Wilson did not hesitate to press Congress for measures that he felt desirable. It is accordingly ironic that the ultimate failure of his career, the Senate's rejection of the League of Nations, was a failure of his relations with the legislative branch.

Other modern Democratic presidents have shown a tendency to extract from Congress every last measure they could. The opening period of Franklin D. Roosevelt's New Deal is the classic example. During the "hundred days," he sent measure after measure to Congress, which dutifully enacted them, sometimes even before printed copies of the bills were available for consideration. Yet like Wilson, Roosevelt ultimately misjudged the limits of what he, as president, could accomplish with Congress. He attempted far too much with his scheme for changing the composition of the Supreme Court and came out severely bloodied and with his reputation impaired. When he sought to intervene in congressional elections in order to defeat his congressional opponents (the "purge" of 1938), the results were so meager as to be a failure.

More recent Democratic presidents may have learned from their predecessors' experiences, but the lessons have in no way diminished their desire to play highly active roles in the legislative process. Harry Truman was obviously in a weaker position than FDR; the war was over, the country's mood was more conservative, the Congress was Republican, and he himself lacked the Roosevelt voice and manner. Yet he made strenuous efforts to get the congressional action he wanted, and when he failed he ran his campaign for reelection, not against the Republican nominee for president, but against the record of the Eightieth Congress, which had obstructed him. It was a successful tactic.

John F. Kennedy was perhaps the most cautious of the Democratic presidents. His short time in office probably exaggerates the impression of caution he left, and his slender margin of electoral victory undoubtedly checked his impulse to action. Yet he was always acutely aware of the difficulties he faced at the opposite end of Pennsylvania Avenue, so aware that he pressed for his program with less vigor than a more insensitive president might have displayed. Despite these limitations of situation and temperament, however, Kennedy had a vision of legislative responsibilities very much like that of his predecessors. In fact, his contribution was probably felt in the successful outcome of Lyndon Johnson's extreme activism with Congress, a forcefulness that has seldom been matched in presidential history.

The recent Republican presidents present a marked contrast. Herbert Hoover had the worst luck of any president since Andrew Johnson. Much of the meagerness of his record must be set down to the brutal fact of the Great Depression and his defeat for reelection. Nevertheless, both by temperament and belief he was ill disposed to place much pressure on Congress. In personality, he had little of the superficial grace and appeal that help disarm opposition. In belief, he was committed to avoiding public action wherever possible; he had a strong distaste for laws and anything that smacked of compulsion. Dwight Eisenhower held an even more rigid view of his role as president. At times, he seemed to envisage an almost absolute separation between the executive and legislative functions: the former were his, but they should in no way intrude upon the functions of Congress. He was, of course, not consistent in this conception—no president could be—but it is certain that he had a very exalted view of the prerogatives of Congress. He endured attacks upon his branch from Wisconsin Senator Joseph McCarthy with a silent patience that astonished his contemporaries. Ultimately, his behavior is traceable only to a belief that a president should not mix in legislative affairs. Richard Nixon had a much less rigidly "Republican" view, but he was less an activist than Lyndon Johnson.

If there are considerable differences in the conceptions of the president's proper role in legislation as held by the major parties and by different presidents, these differences are of degree, relating only to the question of *how active* the president should be in the legislative process. Even President Eisenhower, who took as extreme a position of presidential passivity vis-à-vis Congress as any modern president, was often a genuine activist in practice. The time is now past when a president can leave lawmaking to the legislators. The modern president is, whether he likes it or not, the chief lawmaker. One fundamental reason for this is, as Edward S. Corwin observed, "the revival of legislation of national scope"—that and the imperative need for it. Behind this need lies the steadily intensifying integration of the nation. In the past, Congress could pass measures designed purely to assist particular regions, states, or localities and could be confident that the effects of the measures would reach only those particular areas. Accordingly, the bulk of legislation was usually left to the bargaining and logrolling of the representatives from the affected areas; thus, questions of reclamation of arid lands were normally left to the senators and congressmen from the western states, cotton matters were placed in the hands of legislators from the cotton states, and so on. Strong tradition still dictates that most legislative problems be handled in this manner. In truth, however, not even cotton and reclamation were ever of such exclusively regional concern as their handling in Congress suggested. The interest shown in such matters by the nationwide environmental movement demonstrates this fact. The nation is more closely knit each year; communications steadily improve, and, both economically and socially, the nation becomes more nearly one. The president, with his unique nationwide constituency, is forced to regard most legislation as national legislation—and to take an active part in its formulation and passage.

The increasing intricacy of national organization of all kinds is paralleled by a similar integration internationally. Accordingly, some of the most important foreign problems requiring legislation have a character that inescapably places them on the president's desk. Although foreign affairs have always been of this nature, they have now taken on such a bewildering complexity that few congressmen or senators can safely devote themselves to acquiring expertise in this area. Even for those few who can, the nature of the problems and the information needed make foreign affairs the peculiar province of the executive branch.

Another such area is monetary policy. This abstruse field is too technical to be carefully monitored by more than a few of the legislative representatives, but all of them have a keen sense of its deep importance to the health of the general economy. Congress has attempted to allocate major responsibility for monetary policy to an independent body, the Federal Reserve Board, where it presumably is invulnerable to presidential or partisan whims. In practice, general monetary policy is managed beyond the effective reach of Congress but not of the president. Closely related to monetary policy in general significance is fiscal (tax) policy. Here, by contrast, Congress has thought of itself as competent and has felt constrained to take an active part. Yet increasingly, as Keynesian economics has gained the day, executive influence has been prominent—and is likely to grow. Much the same is true in such areas as military matters and scientific policy. Congress may react in dismay from time to time, but the legislative branch is inevitably in an inferior position compared with the executive. And the president is the chief executive.

Important as the changes resulting from the increasing complexities of modern life are, the deep and subtle change that has come over the government itself is even more important. It is a form of technological change. To understand it, it is necessary to look back a number of decades. Until the end of World War I, there was nothing that could be taken as a general plan of government programs and operations. Congress, jealously guarding its duties and prerogatives on taxing and spending, passed bills and appropriations separately, without regard to the relationship of each piece of legislation to the other, a practice that, in a business firm or a household, would soon bring disaster. Although not disastrous to the nation, it was costly and wasteful. In 1921 a fundamental reform of American government was instituted by the Budget and Accounting Act. Although the major impetus was the drive to bring expenditures and income into some sensible relationship to each other, the long-term importance of the act was more far-reaching. It called upon the president to prepare an annual budget to present to Congress. Even though Congress undertook to neither accept the budget nor refrain from tampering with it (in practice the legislators have proved ready to make large-scale changes), passage of the act was a profound admission that that body was incapable of serving this fundamental function of government. Therefore, the job went where it had to rest, to the executive branch.

Effective reform, however, was years in the making. The Bureau of the Budget was only gradually able to do more than collect and add up the various separate demands for money and tabulate the various sources of income. Moreover, until 1939, when it was placed in the Executive Office of the President, the budget bureau was located in the Treasury Department. The new location and the growing competence and prestige of the bureau not only enhanced its power but markedly increased the president's capability. This increased capability extended to most parts of government in one degree or another— and gave the president a great advantage over Congress. He now had a basic tool for making the executive branch his own (as the Constitution indicated it should be, but as previous practice had never allowed). Congress could still change particular features of the president's governmental plan and enforce its own authority over particular agencies, but the budget, increasingly the president's plan, was the starting point.

Over the years it has become apparent that the creation of the Bureau of the Budget was no mere administrative reform directed at housekeeping tidiness; it was a governmental change of constitutional importance. A fundamental device for coordinating policy, it placed both power and responsibility for policy on the president. The change effected was not apparent during World War II, a period in which executive leadership in legislation was to be expected anyhow, or even immediately afterward. In 1946, for example, the complaint was heard that there was no legislative program coming from the president: presidential reports and recommendations, yes, but no presidential legislative program as such. Later, under President Truman, however, just such a program took form, and under President Eisenhower, who often seemed to defer to Congress in his general statements, the formulation of a president's program became both routinized and accepted.

With the new Republican administration firmly established after some inevitable initial groping, the Bureau of the Budget, acting in the president's name, sent instructions in mid-1954 to all the federal agencies calling upon them to submit legislative plans according to a standard form. Out of the intense scrutiny of the resulting mass of agency proposals by the top leadership of the new Republican administration, the president's legislative program emerged. As Richard Neustadt observed, the development of this program was less an innovation by President Eisenhower than the product of bureaucratic momentum, which carried on a beginning made during the previous administration. It was also the natural evolution of the change that started in 1921. President Nixon carried the evolution a step further, recognizing and increasing the managerial responsibilities of this agency and renaming it the Office of Management and Budget (OMB), a development to which Congress responded by creating its own Congressional Budget Office.

Although this change to OMB is of much importance to the character of the American governmental system, it should not be regarded as a total transformation. As we have seen, it was in progress for more than four decades and involved both Republican and Democratic administrations. And although the trend is quite clear retrospectively, the president and the executive branch have not reduced Congress to a rubber stamp in the monetary field. When a great majority in Congress is of the same party as the president, as after the election in 1964, the president may briefly have his way to a striking degree. This situation is inevitably short-lived, however; party discipline is weak, and even the highly touted persuasive powers of a Lyndon Johnson cannot long maintain harmony between Congress and the president—or, as some would put it, cannot long keep Congress subservient to the president. Moreover, a shrewd president will inevitably tailor his program to what he conceives is possible; he may desire much more far-reaching legislation than he sends to Congress, but he will certainly have no desire to incur a series of defeats that may damage his prestige.

Despite this ground for presidential caution, however, the fact remains that an important change has occurred. There has been a gradual but widespread acceptance of the concept of a presidential program of legislation. Although it is understood that the formulation of measures must take place in the individual agencies of the executive branch, it is now also accepted that the important measures of the president's program should be drafted in the OMB, which has particularly competent facilities for this function. This is far from saying that Congress will accept the measures, or even accord them a high degree of respect. At the same time, Congress has become reluctant to pass measures that touch on subjects of interest to the president but do not have executive support. Leading senators and representatives will even on occasion refer proposed measures to the executive branch for initial decision and possible bill drafting. This is a major departure from the traditional notion of how the separation of powers operates.

Although there is no single formal presentation of the president's legislative program to Congress, each year a number of highly important general messages go from the president to the legislative branch. The first is the State of the Union Message, the only regular message called for in the Constitution. It provides the president with an opportunity to discuss general matters, to outline his program, and, if he desires, to dramatize it by making a personal appearance before the two houses. It is not the proper vehicle for laying bare the details of all the measures he will propose; those he sends to Congress later. A second presentation is the Budget Message, which is accompanied by the massive volume containing the budget itself. A third is the Economic Report, which dates from passage of the Employment Act of 1946, a measure whose full importance is just now becoming apparent.

That act, which was based on the deep change in economic thinking associated with the name of John Maynard Keynes, made it a matter of national policy to maintain the national economic health as measured by employment. Accompanied by the Report of the Economic Advisors, the Economic Report states the major economic problems facing the nation and indicates the thinking underlying the administration's general economic policy. Since 1970 the president has also been required to submit an annual Environmental Quality Report; it may come to rival the others in importance. There are several other messages, special in the sense of covering particular topics but general in that they do not detail the various measures that will follow. During the first few months of a new session, Congress may well feel that it is being loaded with an overwhelming agenda by the president.

If the president sets much of the agenda of Congress, what follows is largely in the hands of the two houses. Each senator and congressman is a power in his own right; he has been elected by his constituents and is responsible directly to them. He is not an appointee of and cannot be removed by the president. However much he may admire the president and believe in his program, each senator and representative feels a more or less strong compulsion to assert his independence and autonomy against the authority of the White House. At times he may appear arrogant or downright cussed, but this is a direct result of his election by a distinct constituency; refusal to assert independence could well be taken as subservience and failure to represent the folks back home. This factor occasionally produces ludicrous results, as when senators address each other as though each were the high plenipotentiary of a proud and haughty nation. Once in a while, this spirit of independence takes such exaggerated form that an individual legislator becomes a veritable wild cell, with disastrous consequences to both government and nation. Fortunately, however, the Huey Longs and the Joseph McCarthys are rare.

Partly because of the autonomy inherent in the position of senator or congressman, many checks have developed to prevent Congress from shattering into bits. Perhaps the most important of these checks is the most general and diffuse—what may be termed the *corporate spirit* of each house. It is very marked in the Senate, which has often been described as a club. A large number of customs and rules, both formal and informal, circumscribe the behavior of the members. Thus, for example, a new member is expected to remain quiet and inconspicuous until sufficient time has elapsed for him to know all the niceties. Similarly, no member is allowed to impugn the motives of the others. There are many such rules, almost all grounded in the common awareness of the possible disastrous results to all if the members exercise their independence to the full. There is, further, a clear understanding that, if any member is to achieve results for his own constituency, he has to gain the support of other members of his house. He cannot afford their hostility and has everything to gain by earning their gratitude. Nor would it be realistic to assume that senators and congressmen lack concern for the national interest.

The other large restraint upon a legislator's independence is the party system. Sometimes, when a popular president elected by a large majority has brought into Congress a substantial number of his own party members on his coattails, the winning party may seem irresistible and sweep all before it in Congress. Apprehensive voices will assert that the American system of government has been destroyed and that inevitably the president, as leader of his party, will enforce strict discipline in Congress and thereby wipe out the separation between the executive and legislative branches. For a time the results may seem to bear out the alarmist cries: this is the way things seemed to Republican critics in the early days of the New Deal and in the years immediately following Johnson's huge victory over Goldwater. At such moments, the American pattern resembles the British, with party discipline placing government power, both executive and legislative, in the hands of the national leader.

Such a picture, however, is seriously overdrawn. The periods during which this situation has prevailed have been few indeed. In 1934 Franklin Roosevelt was able to have his way with Congress, not merely because he had so many fellow Democrats in Congress, but because the country was in a state of crisis. In any clear and obvious crisis, partisans of both labels rally behind the president as the national leader. Despite the astonishing growth of the Democratic majority that occurred in the election of 1936, however, a growth directly attributable to the popularity of the president, relations between president and Congress nevertheless became decidedly sticky. There followed the 1938 "purge" attempt, a venture after whose effects cooperative relations between the two branches were restored only by the new crisis of World War II. As for the fears of presidential domination supposedly inherent in the "consensus" proclaimed by President Johnson and apparently authenticated by Congress after his victorious sweep in the election of 1964, their substance related mainly to the Vietnam War. Legislative subservience otherwise began to erode, and when the president undertook to manipulate Congress too blatantly to gain approval of his war policies, the subservience all but vanished.

Party discipline in the United States is a presidential weapon of limited reliability. Only occasionally can a president successfully appeal to his own party's congressional organization to gain passage of measures otherwise doomed. As with almost any weapon, efficacy of discipline depends on its being used sparingly and reserved for that peculiar category of presidentially supported measures, the "must" bills. In the two houses of Congress, party discipline is really quite weak, sometimes nonexistent. Moreover, the party organization in Congress, although it carries the name of the president's party, of which he is the official leader, is not the president's own organization. It is quite capable of dragging its feet, and the president must frequently cajole or even threaten it; the threats are likely to be indications of desperation. One scholar, James M. Burns, has suggested that the congressional party organizations and the organizations headed by the president and his opposing party leader are so distinct that we have in effect four rather than two national parties, two of them presidential and two congressional. Although a president cannot always rely on members of his own party for consistent support of his program in Congress, frequently members of the opposition come to his support. President Eisenhower often benefited from the aid given by Senate Democratic Leader Lyndon Johnson; Presidents Kennedy and Johnson similarly benefited from the help of Senate Republican Leader Everett M. Dirksen.

If such relationships are measured against a British model in which the government governs and the opposition opposes, we have chaos indeed. But the British model is not wholly relevant to American political reality. No American president expects to dominate Congress, nor does the machinery exist for him to do so; certainly party organization is very poorly adapted for such an attempt. A senator or congressman probably owes only a small debt to the president or the national party organization for his election. The party organization that participates in the election of a senator or a congressman (if, indeed, one exists) is a local or a state organization. Central party organizations may provide money for particular congressional candidates facing crisis, but for the most part resources must be found locally. On the whole, these candidates have little reason to be grateful to or to depend on national party organizations. And they are unable to forget that each of their electorates is different from the next, most of all from that which chooses a president. After election, the candidates elected under the same party banner as the president may feel a share in the glory surrounding his name, but time quickly dulls the sense of obligation, and the competing obligation to the demands of the particular constituencies asserts itself. The initial cohesiveness of the winning party loosens, and the president finds that his party's congressional battalions are no longer his to command. They may actually be a check upon him.

In dealing with Congress, indeed with virtually all of government, every president inevitably and repeatedly collides with another feature of American political life—a multitude of organizations, some formal and some informal, each clustered about particular matters of policy or potential policy. It is the modern form of what James Madison termed the problem of "faction." Lobbying is the aspect of the problem that has received most attention. Presidents have always been vexed by the persistent and importuning influences of lobbyists seeking to gain their ends at the expense of presidential policy. In 1913 President Wilson, for example, denounced the horde of lobbyists who descended on Washington at the first whisper of new tariff legislation. Other presidents have echoed him, and not just on tariff matters. Though the activities of some lobbyists have on occasion assisted presidential programs, and though a function of White House staff assistants is to act as lobbyists (or, more politely, to serve as liaison with Congress), lobbyists have generally helped frustrate presidential ends.

Lobbying, however, is only one aspect of the problem, and certainly not the most important. Lobbying is in itself not wrong, nor, indeed, is it something to which a president can properly take exception. The First Amendment to the Constitution guarantees the right to petition the government for a redress of grievances. Congress and the executive branch both would be severely handicapped if they could not draw on information and opinion from the citizenry. Moreover, the vision of congressmen as passively responding to whatever pressures the lobbyists for "special interests" bring to bear is quite mistaken. While no congressman would say that he ignores the appeals of lobbyists, all congressmen would indignantly reject any suggestion that they simply yield to pressure.

The real problem is quite different. Whether pressure is effective or not, it is usually unnecessary. Each congressman (and, to a lesser extent, each senator) is chosen by and represents a constituency that is smaller than the president's. Necessarily, the congressman's constituency has less diversity than the president's. In some areas, it includes little more than a single preponderant economic interest—a particular farm commodity or industry. In such a constituency or in one with few interests, there is little point in applying pressure on the elected representative; he will be keenly aware of the situation and may be relied upon to seek advice from the interest in question. Such a congressman is not a true lobbyist, though he is more effective than most lobbyists in accomplishing his ends. As a consequence, the producers of cotton, oil, apples, airplanes, and many other products have especially good representation in Congress. In a national context, however, the voices of individual interests are much less resounding, and often their echoes are drowned out in the competing clamor of the others.

Though there are great differences in the preoccupations of different congressmen and senators, to a large degree these preoccupations do not conflict. Accordingly, nothing stands in the way of cooperative exchange of support for each others' projects—in short, logrolling. The process is best typified by the rivers and harbors bills regularly passed by Congress. One congressman's concern may be limited to obtaining a levee for his district, while another may care only for a dam for *his* district, and so on. In order to gain their individual ends, they vote for each others' bills. The general consequence is likely to be a vast miscellany of projects unrelated to each other or, indeed, to the national interest. This process is repeated many times over in each legislative session; it produces peace among the most vociferous and powerful interests as well as among the legislators. It does not, however, meet the need for coherent plans of policy in public works, taxation, foreign affairs, or many other areas where the president is obliged by his mandate to take a large view.

To a substantial degree, the organization within Congress is based upon the mutual accommodation of a variety of wholly separate interests. Such organization, though shifting with the needs and chances of alliance and support, is real and is, on the whole, antagonistic to the very conception of a presidential program. It tends to elevate interests and values that are more solidly organized and more surely founded on the accidents of legislative district boundaries. This form of organization goes beyond the houses of Congress and includes particular agencies and bureaus of the executive branch as well as private organizations. Though often transitory, it can be durable. These systems of power are reinforced by the committees of Congress, which tend to give inordinate power over certain fields of policy to congressmen from districts where those interests are especially strong. A president who proposes to challenge any of these systems must be either very strong or very reckless.

Given this situation, the possibilities for presidential action involving Congress are severely limited. To evaluate a president on the basis of the number of bills passed that were sponsored by him may impart the kind of objectivity that comes with citing numbers. In a large sense, however, it is a false measure. Any politician acute enough to have risen to the presidency is keenly aware of the obstacles to his program in Congress. He will accordingly cut his program to the possibilities. While one president may, like Lyndon Johnson, have an unusual skill in persuasiveness and legislative generalship, his achievement will be only marginally enhanced by these attributes. Much, probably most, of what a president does not achieve with Congress consists of what he does not attempt. And for this there is no satisfactory measure.

Moreover, the achievement of a president in producing changes through legislative action is also understated by any tabulation of bills passed—or not passed—in any one session. Although measures that require legislative sanction are usually important, they are not all equally important. And the major items of change are not usually accomplished in any single session of Congress. Final action on a particular measure is only the culmination of a process begun many years before and probably including defeats of earlier bills to the same end. Most of the really important legislation that has made history in recent years thus originated in earlier studies, education, and herculean effort—even decades before. The National Labor Relations Act and the acts establishing or guaranteeing social security, civil rights, and medicare are examples. A president who sponsors an important innovation but does not see it enacted in his own time may have made a greater contribution than the president under whose leadership it actually becomes law.

Although the fate of the president's legislative program is the most conspicuous index of the relations between president and Congress, other aspects are also important. One is the degree of cooperation on foreign policy, an area peculiarly within the presidential sphere but one for which Congress shares responsibility, notably by virtue of the Senate's constitutional power to approve treaties. The Senate's rejection of American participation in the League of Nations will be vivid for years to come. It is doubtful that the Senate will again so repudiate a president, partly because no president, recalling that event, would expose himself as Woodrow Wilson did, but partly because the Senate is unlikely to court the risks to the nation that comparable action in today's dangerous world might involve. Although a prudent president involves influential senators in the formulation—and sometimes the execution—of major steps in foreign affairs, the Senate today has less power in foreign affairs than it had in the past.

Congress is also capable of making life miserable for officials of the executive branch on whom the president may heavily depend. This is most likely to occur to the president's own assistants in the White House establishment. These individuals are appointed without congressional review and engage in activities that are almost necessarily hidden from public view. Moreover, to the degree that they are in frequent contact with the president, they are likely to exercise considerable power. Responsible only to the president and perhaps seemingly indispensable to him, these aides recurrently arouse hostility in congressional and other breasts. This occurred with Sherman Adams, chief assistant to President Eisenhower, and even more with H. R. Haldeman and John Ehrlichman, assistants to President Nixon.

The doctrine of "executive privilege" is the chief device available to protect such assistants from responding to questioning that might cause embarrassment or worse to them and their superiors. This doctrine, however, has very ambiguous standing. On the one hand, there is nothing explicit in the Constitution to support it, and, as the last days of the Nixon administration showed, it is open to serious abuse in covering up executive misdeeds. On the other hand, there is danger to the nation itself if all discussions in the White House are to be opened to public scrutiny; the effect could well be a loss of the frank and honest advice a president must have. As a result, while the doctrine will always arouse suspicion when asserted, it is unlikely to be completely repudiated. In any event, it is a dubious protection for presidential aids under attack in Congress; the experience mentioned above suggests that the ultimate presidential solution to such a problem is the enforced resignation of the assistants. And Richard Nixon's own experience indicates that in extremity the doctrine will not save a president either.

In the guerrilla conflicts that occasionally develop between president and Congress, there are thus formidable weapons on each side. The Senate under the Constitution has the power to pass on many important presidential appointments. Refusal to approve such an appointment is an obviously hostile step that the Senate is reluctant to take. Yet this happens; the successive rejection of two Nixon nominees to the Supreme Court is the most extreme example of such action in recent history. Congress can also curtail appropriations—or attach repugnant conditions to them—for programs dear to a president's heart, but this is an almost normal problem for any president.

A president, on the other hand, holds the constitutional power to veto measures passed by Congress. Even in the hands of so mild a president as Gerald Ford, the veto power is a strong weapon. Congress, of course, may override the veto—if it can muster the votes of two-thirds of both houses, not an easy thing to do. Nevertheless, indiscriminate or too frequent use of the veto can bring retaliation. The president also controls some appointments of great interest to members of Congress. Usually "courtesy" demands that such members of Congress be "consulted" (that is, deferred to) in these appointments, but sometimes presidents use the appointments as weapons against maverick legislators. Much the same thing can be done with the location of defense plants and the placing of important contracts. A president may "impound" money appropriated by Congress, that is, refuse to spend it. Nixon was checked by the courts in his extreme use of this device, but it has not been outlawed as such. A president may also make a stirring television appeal over the heads of Congress directly to the electorate, a tactic that loses effectiveness if used too often. All these devices risk deepening hostilities with Congress and so can only be used with restraint.

In one sense, impeachment is the ultimate stage of conflict between Congress and the president. While it is true that the Constitution gives the House of Representatives power to bring charges against a president and the Senate power to try him, the process involves far more than a simple contest between two branches of government. It is a culmination of political crisis that goes to the heart of the national consensus. Only two presidents, Andrew Johnson and Richard Nixon, have been confronted with such proceedings. Johnson escaped conviction by one vote, but the circumstances of the trial were so flawed that it seemed afterward that so drastic a procedure would be unlikely in the future. Accordingly, a long and agonizing national ordeal had to be endured and strong evidence of criminal behavior assembled before the House Judiciary Committee was able to vote an impeachment resolution against Nixon. He resigned. One consequence is certainly that impeachment remains an operative part of the Constitution, but another may well be that, because of the ordeal experienced in reaching the point of impeachment in this case, such proceedings may be even more difficult to institute in the future.

The relationship between the president and Congress is considerably different from that formally drawn in the great scheme of the Constitution. The separation of powers between these two branches has not indeed been removed; a wide gap separates the two. Nevertheless, the increasing complexities of modern political life have required an increasing role for the president, and the presidency has increasingly become institutionalized. Correlatively, the legislative branch has become less and less capable of mastering the daily flow of events of which policy is so largely composed; it is compelled to leave much to the executive branch. If present trends were to be projected into the future, we could envision a governmental system in which the president, with the whole executive branch under his effective control, governs, and Congress checks and criticizes. Already, this picture accords with what happens in some areas of policy, military and foreign affairs especially.

But this has not yet become a general pattern, and it is far from clear that it ever will. Congress wields an enormous and active power. The manner of selecting its membership inevitably leads it into differences and occasionally into collision with the presidency. Though Congress may be more and more handicapped by a growing gap of information and expertise in confrontations with the executive branch and may find increasing difficulty in intelligently checking the actions of government, its capacity for checking and interfering does not seem likely to disappear. If this prospect presents serious danger in the future, it can be mitigated by restrained and responsible statesmanship on both sides.

The principal problem of the relationship between the president and Congress continues to be what it has consistently been through most of American history—the difference between the constituent bases of the two. The one branch will persistently be drawn to look at the common needs of the nation as a whole, and the other will be just as persistently compelled to look to the particular wants of parts of the nation. The perennial danger is not simple presidential domination of the legislative branch. Rather, "it is because in their hours of timidity the Congress becomes subservient to the importunities of organized minorities that the president comes more and more to stand as the champion of the rights of the whole country." The author of this radical statement was that well-known presidential tyrant, Calvin Coolidge.

President and Executive

chapter four

*T*he president is the chief executive. The basis for this statement is found in the clear and forthright opening of Article II of the Constitution, "The executive power shall be vested in a president of the United States of America," and in the injunction that he shall take care that the laws be faithfully executed. These provisions, and a common and oversimplified view of the separation of powers, conjure up a vision of American government in which Congress passes the laws and the president, commanding his subordinates, executes them. The vision is seriously mistaken as to what actually happens in the passage of laws, and it is equally inaccurate as to what happens in their execution. The reality, in fact, is so complex that it is now often difficult to speak meaningfully about "the executive branch." Not only does that branch, as we have seen, take significant leadership in legislation, but it is so divided and fragmented and its parts are often so autonomous that the president's power of command over them is often little more than a fiction. On the other hand, if checks upon presidential power are sought, they can be found as readily among these fragments as in Congress.

The powers of the president under the Constitution are great but at many points imprecisely defined. The courts have been reluctant to define his power more sharply; the courts, after all, are themselves the third of the great branches supposedly coordinate under the separation of powers. Nevertheless, a handful of decisions has placed some limitations on what presidents may do. The most dramatic of these was the *Youngstown* decision of 1952; it compelled President Truman to undo the seizure of the steel mills by which he intended to prevent a threatened strike by the steelworkers. Truman assumed that he had power of seizure under ambiguous legislation in combination with his general responsibilities as president. His position emphasized the great discretionary power inescapable in the presidency, and the Supreme Court felt obliged to strike down what seemed a dangerous claim. Even with this seemingly straightforward action, however, the meaning and long-term effect of the decision are still disputed. In a notable case of 1890, *In re Neagle*, the existence of a fundamental power in the presidency to do what is necessary for the "execution" of the laws, here to insure the personal safety of judges, was affirmed but under such complicated circumstances and in such terms as to leave a deep uncertainty as to how far that power might reach. And, as already noted, the power of "impoundment" has been restricted, but with unclear consequences as to how far the restriction extends.

Probably the most important "executive" power of the president in our modern bureaucratized era is his power to direct the vast machinery of the executive branch. The courts have provided a few limitations, one of the more important of these relating to the president's power of removal of federal officials. This authority seems part of the power to command or direct and flows from the vesting of the "executive power" in the president. It is clearly established, however, that the president may not easily remove a member of the important independent regulatory commissions. But the greatest limitation on this power comes from other sources. The most important is the major extension of the merit civil service. Federal employees under this system, the overwhelming majority of all public servants, can be removed only for narrowly prescribed offenses, and these do not include simple presidential displeasure. The threat of removal is largely meaningless anyhow, given the need for maintaining public services and the dependence of government on the expertise of officials.

There remains a very serious problem of maintaining responsibility of government in the executive branch. The president is the single elective official (except for the vice-president) in the executive branch and is the essential medium of responsibility. Where law prescribes precisely what public servants must do or when there are standards of practice either of long standing or derived from scientific findings, the president is largely absolved from blame if the results prove unpopular. Yet many actions clearly rest on value decisions by administrators. These value decisions are choices—preferences—that have to stand as such. Who is to get the benefits and who the deprivations flowing from such decisions? What kind of benefit is to be chosen, material or nonmaterial? Where such choices are mixed into the decisions of administration—and they are much more frequently than administrators usually care to admit—they must be justified somehow as reflecting the choices of the people themselves and not simply as being those personally preferred by the officials. Since an appointive administrator has his only formal link with the people via his political superiors and finally the chief executive, the president is crucial in the formal scheme of responsible government, especially as the complexities of modern life require more of these decisions to be made by administrators.

In practice, an administrator faced with an important decision that reflects a choice between values or between different interests will attempt to protect himself against the wrath of those who might feel injured by his choice. He may disguise the existence of personal preference in his decision and insist that purely technical considerations prevail; he may try to assess the sentiment of the people most obviously affected; certainly he will give thought to the relative strength of the various groups involved. In doing all this, he may establish some more or less formal means of consultation—an advisory committee, a conference, or some other device. The result is hailed as the work of "democratic" administration, but the main end of the process is to protect exposed administrators fearful of facing a legitimate charge of arbitrary behavior in exercising their own preferences. By mobilizing the support of those groups that benefit from their decisions, administrators at least assure themselves of effective friends when attacks develop. This form of politics, often more important than the contests between parties, involves ties among administrators within the executive branch, representatives and senators, and organized interest groups. Here is a pattern of responsibility even where the president is not actually in control of all the many agencies that are nominally under his command and part of the executive branch of which he is the constitutional head. This, however, is responsibility to a segment rather than to the whole of the public.

Thus, there are many ways that bureaucracy is held responsible to the people for its actions. One is the fundamental requirement that actions be based on law, including court decisions, congressional statutes, and constitutional requirements. When the provisions of law become unsatisfactory to the public, there are ways of changing them. A second means lies in the professional competence of the civil servants—their adherence to the objective standards of their professions, whatever specialties they practice. A third is their obedience to their political superiors in the executive establishment, ultimately to the president, the elective head and formal link to the electorate. A fourth is the array of largely informal systems of direct consultation with parts of the public and its representatives. Basic to all these safeguards is the fact that the bureaucracy in America is not a special mandarin caste but an open body of public servants from most parts of American society who generally share the values and tastes of that society.

The role of the presidency is nevertheless critical. Although most civil servants can be relied upon to stay within the laws by which their activities are ruled, the existence of a system of hierarchy with clear authority at the top is an important insurance of legal observance. Moreover, since reference to law and science cannot actually determine all the value choices that must be made if government is to operate, some reference to the public is necessary. This leaves much of the problem to the various systems of informal consultation that agencies have worked out with the groups and individuals most directly involved, or to the president and his own appointees. But between these last two possibilities there are important differences. While the systems of bureaucratic consultation are able to take into account the wishes of the groups directly consulted, they are less able to weigh the interests of those who are indirectly affected and those who are less vocal or less informed. Moreover, the individual agencies usually have close associations with the directly affected groups (their "clientele"). The president, on the other hand, is responsible to the whole electorate and can have no special ties to any one group. The formal system of bureaucratic responsibility that culminates in his office accordingly has to care for those groups and individuals indirectly affected by the actions of the many bureaus and agencies.

The magnitude of this presidential responsibility is difficult to picture. Though the number of civilians on the federal payroll fluctuates, it has been as high as 2.5 million people; of these, approximately 30,000 are in the legislative and judicial branches, the others in the executive. This horde of people is distributed among a bewildering number of departments, government corporations, agencies, and bureaus. By one count, there are something more than 1,800 divisions, branches, offices, and other subunits in the executive branch. Few of the specialized skills of modern man are not represented among their activities. Yet this is the establishment that the president must direct and in some sense hold accountable to the people of the United States.

Even if the executive branch were purely patterned after a military model, which it is not, the problem of gaining simple obedience to the president's direction would be enormous. There would not only be ordinary failures of communication and honest misunderstandings but, on occasion, willful confusion and indulgence of cross-purposes. Some goals would be unwittingly assigned to different units, and others would be unassigned. Many decisions would be based on wrong information—and some on very nearly none at all. Such difficulties are common in any large organization and at best can only be minimized, never eliminated. They certainly occur in the federal bureaucracy.

Built into the federal bureaucracy, moreover, is a whole series of obstacles to presidential influence, chief among them being inertia, a tendency to go on doing what has always been done. This is the consequence, not merely of habit and an impulse to "play it safe," but of an endless list of rules and procedures designed for the admirable purpose of eliminating personal whim and preference. Though this "red tape" genuinely protects citizens against favoritism and corruption, it also implies an established way of doing things and, often, particular policies. This may be well and good as long as the established ways and policies are appropriate, but it can be enormously frustrating when change is attempted.

An essential part of any president's undertaking is to place his own people—persons who see things his way and will consult with him on critical questions of policy—in posts of control in the vast bureaucratic mechanism. These individuals are "political appointees," that is, not subject to the normal procedure of selection by competitive examination. It is entirely right that there should be such appointees; these are the people who will decide important policy and will be responsible to the president and, through him, to the American people for the consequences. When in the eyes of the public or of the president they fall short, he can ask for their resignations and replace them. They are usually people with the special quality of sensitivity to public desires and moods that all able politicians must have. But should only department heads and that general category of posts for which the consent of the Senate is necessary be appointed in this way? How can a lonely bureau chief, as the sole presidential representative in the bureau, hope to control a functioning organization sufficiently to know what is going on and to be able to seize the initiative on matters of policy? How far down the ranks is it necessary to place such appointees?

An administration long in office is tempted to reduce severely the number of such appointees and to establish important policy-determining posts as professional civil service jobs. In this way, policies that the incumbent president and his administration are interested in can be placed beyond easy later challenge. The temptation of a new administration and a new president, on the other hand, is to increase the number of political appointees and so make a change of direction easier. The issue became acute in 1953, when a Republican administration succeeded the Democrats after twenty years, during which there had been profound innovations of policy. President Eisenhower had promised a whole new direction of policy, but he found that taking control of the cumbersome bureaucratic behemoth of which he was the nominal head and turning it in a new direction seemed almost impossible. His increase in the number of posts labeled political brought cries from Democrats that Mr. Eisenhower was undermining the civil service system. The problem of maintaining responsibility of government that he thus attempted to solve was nonetheless real.

President Nixon, even more suspicious of civil servants than Eisenhower, undertook much more drastic measures. These included an attempted radical reorganization of the major departments, the creation of a very rigidly centralized White House staff, a strengthened Budget Bureau (rechristened OMB), and the placing of more than 100 members of his White House staff, personal assistants, and former campaign workers in key positions in the executive branch. This "New American Revolution," as he proclaimed it, together with his attempts to negate established programs by impoundment and other means, evoked a widespread reciprocal mistrust within the bureaucracy; it was "guerrilla warfare," as John Ehrlichman described it. It helped precipitate resistance both inside and outside the government that forced abandonment of the reorganization and undoubtedly provoked many of the leaks of information that kept the Watergate scandal alive. It was an unwitting demonstration that even a president cannot operate a government on the basis of deep mistrust.

In a very fundamental sense the problem of directing the "machinery" of government is a *political* problem. Simple command is not enough, and neither is reliance on the loyalties of a president's own personal followers. There is a genuine necessity to enlist as appointees individuals who have their own political support. Inevitably, however, there are not enough such political leaders who are also close supporters of a president to fill all the posts that control the bureaucratic machine. A president will have to appoint some whom he knows slightly or not at all. He will also have accumulated political debts to political leaders and groups that supported him in his campaign, who may expect certain appointments to go according to their wishes. Even a president in office for some time needs the support of some groups to carry out major projects. Appointments to office— patronage in a sense, but at a high level—are essential devices of the political art. The difficulty is that the ends of exercising bureaucratic control and acquiring political support are often mutually exclusive. A political appointee to the Department of Agriculture, say, recommended by a large farm organization that has supported the president, cannot readily be removed. Nor can he be expected to be simply the president's man in the executive. He is a political officer in his own right, rather as if he had won office by election.

If establishing and maintaining control is difficult, knowing how to use it and for what ends is yet more so. A president is not a specialist, yet he must take action on the basis of the most abstruse information. Gaining the services of the very ablest specialists that the nation affords is not a major problem; a call from the president of the United States is very nearly impossible to refuse. But who are the experts, and which of them should be called? Next, having selected his experts, what is the president to make of their advice? They may disagree. Or they may give advice that, for perhaps indefinable reasons, arouses his doubts: he may sense that mixed with the technical judgment are private preferences and biases. Perhaps no more serious recent example of this has occurred than in President Kennedy's decision to approve the venture at the Bay of Pigs in 1961. The operation had been started before Kennedy came to office; he was presented with the plans before he had an opportunity to assess his advisers. The military strongly advised going ahead with the well-advanced undertaking; failure, he was told, was highly unlikely. With some reluctance he assented. The results were disastrous. Presidents Johnson and Nixon have had their own reasons for mistrusting expert military advice; repeatedly in Vietnam the successes promised from particular forms of escalation did not materialize. Nor is the military field the only area in which experts need be listened to with caution.

The resources of manpower and organizational machinery at the disposal of the president are not large. As we have seen, controlling the military and the vast number of civil servants is itself no small part of his problem. The number of people whom he can know personally is limited; even a president can count on no more than twenty-four hours in a day. When he places his own men in key posts, he must expect that, despite all the goodwill and loyalty on their part that could be hoped for, their jobs will require them to see things in a perspective different from his. A high official of the Department of the Interior, for example, cannot be effective in his own job and concurrently sensitive to how a decision, say, on matters of oil affects national defense and the long-term conduct of foreign relations. Perspectives will differ, properly, and a president may be wise to ask no more of his friend at Interior than that he be a genuine advocate of the views of his department; it will be the president's responsibility to relate such views to other considerations.

For assistance in his own job, the president relies upon a handful of men attached to his office who are not specialists like those found in the departments and operating agencies. Even here, he has to accept limitations. Perhaps the first officer who comes to mind as a potential high-level presidential assistant is the vice-president. Many times have presidents announced that the vice-president would henceforth have important responsibilities; each time, however, it somehow works out that the vice-president is not a key figure in the administration, and the office is still regarded with mild amusement. The primary reason is that the vice-president is not simply the president's man: he is the potential successor to the president. There is latent tension between a man and his possible heir. Although vice-presidents have been given important functions not assigned them by the Constitution and can give material help to their chiefs, frustration is almost inevitable while they are in office; certainly presidents are unlikely to treat them as seconds-in-command.

The cabinet also suffers from the same fundamental handicap that minimizes the office of vice-president: the Constitution assigns the executive power very simply to the president. Some cabinet members may be important political figures in their own right and so feel themselves entitled to a careful hearing from the president; when they do not receive this, as, for example, Secretary of the Interior Walter Hickel did not from President Nixon, resignation is indicated. Others are not so entitled, however, and may in fact be overshadowed by some of the bureau chiefs nominally under them. Like the vice-president, they are on hand for the consideration of large decisions only on the call of the president. Some presidents have made effective use of their cabinets and have sought to benefit from the collective wisdom of the members; others, however, among them John F. Kennedy, have not troubled to call many cabinet meetings. Ultimately, the American cabinet has no genuine collective responsibility and has, as one scholar has put it, only a "symbolic value."

Since World War II the Executive Office has grown steadily in importance under all presidents. President Nixon gave it particular attention, attention that has endowed it with prestige and power at the expense of the regular departments, most notably the State Department. Not all its staff, however, are equally important, since it may include a number of agencies, such as the Office of Telecommunication Policy and the Office of the Special Representative for Trade Negotiations, that are hardly to be ranked with the Office of Management and Budget and the Central Intelligence Agency, also parts of the Executive Office. Some of the agencies in the office are clearly staff aids to the president. Others, such as the Office of Economic Opportunity and the Special Action Office for Drug Abuse Prevention, have occasionally been so located as much to dramatize presidential concern in fields of particular urgency as to give the president assistance. Only a small number of individuals in the Executive Office are genuinely close to the president.

During the first few years of the New Deal, the whirlwind of events about the White House produced a condition approximating institutional apoplexy. One of the most important studies of the administrative system ever undertaken, that of the Brownlow Committee, proclaimed that "the president needs help." Roosevelt generally lacked a staff of his own, and the nation suffered as a consequence. The president, therefore, was given help in the form of a group of assistants with (in the words of the Brownlow Committee) "a passion for anonymity." This seemingly small and obvious reform has been vital to the effective operation of the modern presidency.

"The passionate anonyms," as Washington wits promptly dubbed them, have not always been inconspicuous. In the Kennedy administration some of them were very colorful figures indeed, and in the Nixon administration virtually the entire staff achieved notoriety. Yet the idea inherent in their posts was that they should be retiring and capable assistants devoted purely to the president.

The danger that this conception sought to avoid first materialized during the Eisenhower administration. Sherman Adams, an unusually competent organizer and former governor of New Hampshire, was the leading presidential assistant and, in effect, a chief of staff within the White House. Consequently, much attention was drawn to him and, having no political support other than the president's, he was highly vulnerable to attack. When it became possible to smear his reputation, he became a source of embarrassment to the president and was forced to resign. The wisdom of obscurity in these posts has accordingly, resulted in the practice of giving the individuals holding them unpretentious titles, such as Assistant to the President and Counsellor to the President. Their number has varied but in the past has been small. Recently, that number has approached fifty. Although the assistants have specialized, most of them must necessarily deal with problems in a number of very large areas and be ready to take assignments on short notice as crises develop.

The president also has several assistants with less general assignments. One is his specialist on foreign policy; others deal with military and scientific affairs. In recent years, particularly during the times of McGeorge Bundy and Henry Kissinger, the foreign policy assistant has been under attack as the operator of an office superior to the State Department. The criticism has no doubt been partly captious, but it does point to a serious problem: if the reins of control are held too tightly, the operating departments may become irresponsible and leave their tasks and functions to the White House. If the reins are held too loosely, however, the departments may be irresponsible because of lack of supervision from the president. There is probably no regular pattern of organization that would prove ideal for all presidents and in all situations. In order to maintain the degree of coordination and capacity for quick action in times of crisis in any one of a multitude of areas, the organizational structure must be flexible and informal. Most of all, it must be attuned to the particular president and his manner of leadership.

The recently regularized provision for a small corps of assistants dedicated to the president may have mitigated the need some presidents have felt for alter egos in the White House. The most well known were Colonel E. M. House, an unusually close assistant to President Wilson, and Harry L. Hopkins, who was perhaps equally close to President Franklin Roosevelt in the later years of his administration. House was a Texas politician who helped gain the presidential nomination for Wilson and then became a personal emissary and adviser of the president. Hopkins was a former social worker and administrator who performed similar functions for Roosevelt. In the eyes of their critics, these men were Svengali figures of sinister and irresponsible power. Certainly, any trusted adviser who sees the President of the United States frequently has great power, but the danger from these men has usually been exaggerated; the president, after all, is responsible to the nation for his actions and is entitled to the most devoted assistance he can find. In House and Hopkins, the two presidents certainly found devoted men. The presidency is at times a notoriously lonely post, as any position of great power must be. However, the more routinized White House establishment of the present day should lessen, if not eliminate, the need for such highly personal assistants as House and Hopkins.

Important as the development of a regular White House staff has been, a change of perhaps greater significance has occurred in recent decades at the level just below the White House—encompassing the other offices grouped into the Executive Office of the president. Though some staffs continue from administration to administration, on the whole they are instruments of presidential control of government, and the critical positions are presidential choices. The National Security Council, given the continuing magnitude of military considerations, has been one of the crucial bodies. Established by statute in 1947, its membership includes the president, the vice-president, the secretary of state, the director of the Office of Emergency Planning, the chief of the Central Intelligence Agency, the chairman of the Joint Chiefs of Staff, and the secretary of defense. Thus, the council has some of the characteristics of the cabinet. Although it is a statutory body, its function and utility depend on the use the president makes of it. During the Eisenhower era, it had a rather formal structure and staff and operated—as the president wished—in a fairly routinized manner. This manner was changed under Kennedy, who had less taste than his predecessor for this degree of depersonalization. Similar variations according to presidential preferences can always be expected. Thus, to deal with domestic issues Nixon established a Domestic Council, a body roughly parallel to the National Security Council and perhaps an indication of his satisfaction with the form.

In some ways, the most important part of the executive establishment is the Office of Management and Budget. The OMB, whose legislative activities were discussed in the last chapter, has thoroughly outgrown any belief that its reason for being is to economize. It is now the president's chief medium for exercising control and maintaining responsibility to the public. This function is the outcome—not yet fully achieved—of years of evolution. One of the landmarks of these years was the transfer in 1939 of the budget office from the Treasury Department to the Executive Office of the President. Through the OMB, the president now has regular machinery for checking on what the many sections of government that make up the executive branch are doing and for attempting to coordinate their efforts in relation to each other and to his own program.

The problem of size is particularly difficult with the OMB, and it points up an inherent problem of the modern presidency. How large an effort should it make? How large should its staff be? In recent years the OMB has not been large as federal agencies go. It would seem that a bigger staff might better allow it to check on all the myriad activities of the federal bureaucracy. Too large an OMB, however, would seriously impair the responsibility and initiative of the operating agencies. The proper size and function of the OMB lies somewhere between a handful of people making only spot checks on the large problems and a large staff duplicating the planning of individual agencies. Finding this optimum, however, is not simple.

Perhaps the measure of the growing influence of the OMB is its prestige and ability to attract individuals of high caliber from all parts of government. The office does not have control of the great federal machine, and perhaps it should not; nevertheless, it is increasingly an essential tool for the president in maintaining responsible bureaucracy.

In one sense, the OMB and the National Security Council (with its staff) represent an institutionalization and depersonalization of the presidency. Both help the president carry out his policies and programs by giving him the control over the executive branch that he would not otherwise have. Nevertheless, they also provide a means by which executive functions might continue even in the absence of the president; they are almost capable of governing on the basis of a sort of professionalized policy independent of the directives given by the voters in presidential elections. Conceivably, a president might become a figurehead and ceremonial figure, and the nightmare of bureaucratic irresponsibility would be a reality. It would be hysterical to proclaim this a present danger, but it is a potential problem.

A rather different, but also very important, development in the office of the president is the Council of Economic Advisors. Created by the Employment Act of 1946, it consists of a group of three economists supported by a small staff. As already noted, this landmark act was founded on the economic analysis of John Maynard Keynes and had as its premise the fundamental obligation of modern government to achieve and maintain full employment. The history of the act and of the council illustrate the proposition that a major policy innovation is not achieved by simple passage of an act of Congress. The act was a large achievement and the outcome of a vast effort, but it represented only one of the many steps on the long road to acceptance of its purposes. The council was established slowly and was even slower in becoming effective. Under Truman it lacked sureness and, above all, reliable access to its single and indispensable constituent, the president. Under Eisenhower it was more forceful, and, though led by men who had grave misgivings about the doctrine that underlay their commissions, it was so influential that its successor members tended to deplore it as having been responsible for a serious slackening in the economy.

With President Kennedy, the Council of Economic Advisors came into its own. Its members were selected and began work even before the new administration took office, and, being articulate, able, and aggressive, with a ready listener for their client, they quickly achieved great stature in the government. Whether because their advice was followed first by Kennedy and then by Johnson, or because of lucky coincidence, the economy performed as predicted when steps based on Keynesian analysis were taken—increased depreciation allowances, a tax cut, and others—and unemployment declined dramatically. The council had important rivals during the Nixon and Ford eras, but it retained sufficient prestige to indicate that it is established as a fundamental tool of government in the United States.

The Council of Economic Advisors has provided a notable increase in the president's ability to manage the economy in the largest sense. With sufficient knowledge of current economic data, the government may act to try to contract or expand aggregate demand for goods and services in the nation so as to reduce unemployment, accelerate growth of the economy, or control inflation. Such actions involve changes in rates and kinds of taxation, in the supply of money and credit, and other devices. Although these actions may affect the distribution of wealth within the nation, the primary focus of the council's advice to the president is the general level of the economy. A president is not, of course, able to turn the economic life of the nation in whatever direction he pleases, but he has a far greater chance of affecting the economy than he had hitherto. Considering that presidents are notoriously held to blame whenever depressions come, this is no inconsiderable gift. The advice given by the council can be mistaken (as it occasionally has been in the past); the advice may also be ignored (as it also has been at times). It depends on how well the advisers have gained the president's confidence and on his willingness and capacity to heed them. The advisers must be technically able, of course, but, like the presidential assistants, they must be in sympathy and rapport with their client. It is overstating the case to say that the council is the economic ideologist of the administration. This denies the technical expertise that recent members have plainly brought to the council. But problems of value preferences are inevitably imbedded in the technical problems, and members must accordingly be the president's men. Even so, the rise of the council has undoubtedly advanced the institutionalization of the presidency.

Somewhat modeled on this body is the Council on Environmental Quality, established by the Environmental Policy Act of 1969. Also part of the Executive Office of the President, it prepares the Environmental Quality Report and advises the president on environmental matters. As awareness of the environmental crisis spreads, this body is likely to become more influential.

This survey of the resources at the direct command of the president suggests that his office has achieved, or is about to achieve, an iron control over the federal behemoth. This is far from the truth; indeed, it is questionable whether the presidency has kept up with the centrifugal tendency of the government. Many parts of the government have a large degree of autonomy within the bureaucratic structure. At the same time, they have frequently become parts of systems of power that include elements of Congress and interest groups outside of government. There are many variants on this pattern and differences of degree among the many subsystems. The significant facts for the presidency, however, are that the bureaus and agencies of the federal government often have their own political sources of support and can act independently of presidential wishes. This condition, well known to most presidents, makes administration a form of politics, one of the most complex and difficult to be found anywhere. In participating, as he must if he is to fulfill his mandate, a president is at a very serious disadvantage.

The most obvious, although not always the most important, illustrations of this problem are the independent regulatory commissions. These bodies are thoroughly anomalous in terms of the classic picture of the separation of powers; indeed, the Brownlow Committee once termed them collectively "a headless fourth branch of government." Intended to be free of "politics," which meant party politics, they make rules and also act as quasi-judicial bodies. Their membership, once appointed, is presumably free from the presidential pressure of potential removal, and the commissioners typically have overlapping terms. Behind their creation was an idea of purely expert, scientific, and impartial administration, but because they must decide on matters of policy for which science has no answers, they confront a serious problem of responsibility. Moreover, some of their activities plainly affect fundamental presidential programs and policies. Thus, for example, President Johnson's general economic policy came into a subdued conflict with the policy of the Federal Reserve Board as enunciated by its chairman, William M. Martin, in early 1966. The board, fearing inflation, raised interest rates, an action within its powers but opposed to the president's general economic policy of the time. Since Mr. Martin was very firm in his position, the president had little choice but to put the best possible face on the situation; as the decision to disagree was amicably announced over television by Mr. Martin and President Johnson, it was plain that Johnson preferred discretion to valor in a contest that he knew he could not win. To ease the inherently difficult problem of coordinating economic policy, the members of President Johnson's Council of Economic Advisors and the members of the Federal Reserve Board would meet regularly for lunch. Friendly discussions may help soften the most severe disagreements, but they cannot really eliminate the general problem, for it goes beyond simple communication and personal friendliness or antagonism. Underlying all the verbal differences are differences of economic philosophy and the support of different constituencies.

The president confronts an essentially similar problem with many other agencies, even when he controls the choice of their chiefs. Thus, agencies in the departments of Agriculture, Commerce, and the Interior notoriously have their own "clienteles" (a word that grossly understates the influence held by the groups in question). A president is formally free, given the consent of the Senate, to appoint whomever he pleases as secretaries of these departments. Ineptly chosen secretaries, however, may find themselves isolated and frustrated in their own departments if they attempt to institute programs unpopular with the clienteles of their departments. Their orders may not be obeyed, delay may become chronic, and they may find themselves attacked by the congressional committees concerned with their fields. Knowing the problem, a president is likely to seek men actively supported by important private interest groups and their spokesmen in Congress. By doing this, however, the president will have yielded any hope of simply ordering his supposed subordinates to do as he wishes. Other methods—and perhaps other ends—will have to suffice.

The problem that presidents confront takes many forms. It is rare for an agency simply to defy presidential authority. The more typical problems relate to coordination of competing or overlapping programs, reorganization of agencies, and establishment of new policies. In all such situations, it is tempting but inaccurate to see merely technical problems of efficient administration; the real issues go far beyond technicalities.

For example, many presidents have been troubled by the fierce undercover contests between the various agencies of the federal government that deal with water projects. Study groups such as the Hoover commissions have emphasized the importance of coordination of these agencies, as have virtually all independent experts on water resource management. Time and again, however, in the Missouri basin, in the Red, White, and Arkansas River watersheds, and in other areas, coordinated planning and development have proved impossible. The reason is that the issues involve not only the power of the several agencies but also diverse interests that regard themselves as the peculiar constituents of various agencies. Different values, such as flood control versus irrigation, and so on, are also involved.

The representative character of many government agencies has often frustrated attempts to achieve a seemingly sensible and obvious reorganization of their structure. The largest such contest came during the New Deal, when President Roosevelt attempted a large-scale reorganization of the executive branch. The struggle was precipitated by the resistance of the Forest Service to transfer from the Department of Agriculture—where it had enjoyed autonomy and generally friendly relations with its lumber industry clientele—to the Department of the Interior, where conservation would clearly have been made a stronger objective. Similar fears of disturbed relationships between agencies and their established constituencies in other fields were mobilized, so that when the issue reached Congress, the opposing coalition was formidable and the plan was emasculated. Although most of the discussion centered on efficient organization, the genuine issues were much larger. Consequently, the political difficulties of making fundamental changes in organization are very great, as all recent presidents have learned.

The problem of establishing a new policy sponsored by the president is equally difficult. Repeatedly, new objectives in fields of federal action already occupied by existing agencies have met great opposition. Thus, when an attempt was made in the 1930s to alleviate rural poverty, it was necessary to create an entirely new agency, the Farm Security Administration (as it ultimately became), although a bureau already existed in the field, the Agricultural Extension Service. The latter, however, had not touched the problem of the rural poor and was supported by various congressmen and by the American Farm Bureau Federation and the agricultural colleges; together, these constituted a power structure that destroyed the Farm Security Administration and its program. The innovation of policy here had to rely on presidential support, but even this in the end was insufficient. A more recent incident involves the effort to improve the quality of water and to control pollution. The purpose was confided to the established U.S. Public Health Service, but ultimately it was necessary to create a new agency. The new agency met prompt resistance. Reorganization seems chronic in this area.

The problem a president confronts as administrator, then, is exceedingly difficult. He cannot simply command. He now has improved means for learning what is going on and for reaching out to the different parts of government for which he cannot escape being held responsible. Nevertheless, he cannot hope to accomplish great change without great effort, and he must tailor his ventures to the total resources of his political power. The administrative part of his task is as political as anything he does. The methods adopted by different presidents necessarily vary with their personalities and, more important, with their political situations and the number of their objectives. Franklin Roosevelt has often been charged with disorderliness of administration and love of chaos. He frequently allowed different administrative leaders to engage in public combat over which agencies should undertake which jobs for which ends by which methods. In the process, he learned a great deal about the distribution of power behind the contenders and consequently often achieved compromises favorable to his own ends. Most presidents, however, have not had his peculiar gifts and have been unwilling to allow the surfacing of so much conflict within their administrations.

For all that administration seems technical and a matter of purely organizational and managerial skills, it is intensely political, for it involves the distribution of benefits and deprivations to different groups and the favoring of some values over others. This is most true at the White House level. Here, as elsewhere in his job, the president must be a leader.

Presidential Leadership

chapter five

The more intensively the power of the presidency is analyzed, the more elusive it becomes. The formal powers granted by the Constitution are negligible by any strict reading of the actual language, and they are often stalemated by the grants to Congress. The vast machinery of the executive branch, far from being a finely tempered instrument under the president's control, is one of his major problems. Yet the reputation of the office remains one of great power; and the reputation is largely justified. To a remarkable degree this power consists of the opportunities for leadership that the office gives.

These opportunities vary enormously, both with the times and with the individual who is president. Somewhere mixed in the whole of presidential history is the element of chance or, as Machiavelli put it, Fortune. Presidents who in some circumstances might have risen to genuine greatness never gained the opportunity. Thus, in different circumstances Theodore Roosevelt might have made a decisive mark on history just because of his personal vigor and his belief in the strenuous life; as it was, his opportunities were few and his actions were less impressive than the noise accompanying them. As one perhaps malicious observer noted, it was Roosevelt's misfortune not to be a war president. Somewhat similarly, John F. Kennedy came to office with a commitment to vigor and a desire to carry through programs of social reform; his slender majority, the existence of a severe balance-of-payments problem, and his brief time in the presidency left him a record of few achievements. Harry Truman, on the other hand, finding himself abruptly projected into the presidency and at first afflicted with a sense of inadequacy, rose to near greatness. Nevertheless, it remains true that the American presidency holds great potentialities, some that may be grasped by any man who manages to reach the office, others by only the strongest and ablest of presidents.

Other than its formal machinery, what are the inherent assests of the office? First, perhaps, is the sheer mystique of the office. The moment the successful candidate has been elected, he becomes a man set apart. His friends cease to address him by his first name, and he is treated everywhere with deference and awe. His every glance and gesture are noted and searched for meaning. His clothes, his books, his pets—these and other features of his private life become matters of triumph or anguish to vociferous professional spokesmen. His most casual strolls are dogged by eagle-eyed protectors, and his children have the unflagging chaperonage of agents from the Secret Service. Seemingly everything about him is reported to the public, and nearly everything is criticized. More thoroughly than anyone else he has lost his privacy. It is as though all the exposure, publicity, and captious criticism of his personal foibles were intended to remind him that he is mortal and not divine.

The aura of grandeur remains, however; no exposure of pettiness or human fallibility can destroy it. Indeed, the attention that hangs upon his every word and all the criticisms are signs that the president combines the symbolic role of chief of state with the substantive one of head of government. Every expectation proclaims that he is a man of power, and at every point the expectation is itself a source of power. Since he is believed to be powerful and since he is symbol of the nation itself, he is often heeded even when reflection indicates that he has no power to compel. Thus, an invitation to the White House, whether for a conference in an industrial crisis or for a reading of poetry, is very nearly a summons. The invitation may indeed be declined, but the refusal is a political act.

The endowment of this power comes with the office, but the

power itself is confined within obscure and indefinable limits, and it can never be used carelessly lest it be diminished. Some presidents have been able to add to it, and others have markedly decreased it. When, for example, a president uses his power to gain a settlement of an industrial dispute, he is likely to find (as President Kennedy did) that its force is roughly proportionate to the infrequency with which he applies it. Used in other than rare and exceptional circumstances, it also weakens the ordinary and mundane processes by which such crises are normally settled. Here is a paradox: the prestige of the presidency and the awe it inspires carry power only to the extent that it is not used. How, then, is prestige a source of power?

The question has no easy answer. Partly, it may be said that the prestige of the office carries real, though limited, power. The limits apply more to frequency of use than to extent. Moreover, its use requires an almost exquisite sensitivity in the president himself. He must know when to invoke prestige and when to reserve it. He must also know how to use it. Since much of its force, like magic, lies in its mystery and its uncertain consequences, it is usually best used in combination with other, more explicit power. That is, prestige is genuinely useful up to the point at which it meets an explicit test; such a test may well destroy it.

There has been no more vivid illustration of this than the 1962 steel crisis. In this incident, President Kennedy committed his prestige to gain agreement by the industry and the union for only moderate increases in prices and wages. His plan called for behavior very different from that of the past. The president and his White House associates felt that they had achieved a dramatic success of industrial diplomacy when the union reluctantly agreed to forgo the advantages it had gained in direct negotiations with the industry and settled for a relatively moderate wage increase. So far, the president, largely by making use of the awe inspired by his office, had succeeded. However, there was a second part of the diplomatic arrangement, which the president thought the industry had accepted: it would refrain from increasing its prices excessively. U.S. Steel, however, having accepted the first part of the implied bargain—a low wage settlement—proceeded to raise prices substantially.

At this point, the president's prestige not only failed to solve the specific problem; it reached the brink of its own destruction for future purposes. Unless the president could now manage to force the industry, as represented by U.S. Steel, to rescind its action, labor would henceforth no longer trust the president and would become more intransigent than ever. The steel industry would also have proved that it had no need to listen to him. Nor would this be the end of the chain of consequences. With the rest of the country and the world watching, others—nations as well as industries—would draw similar conclusions. How far the results might reach would be unforeseeable, but certainly they might prove disastrous. The president had taken an enormous gamble, probably without perceiving what the stakes were, and he faced an abyss.

Now fully aware of his peril, President Kennedy went into a whirlwind of activity. Everything that anybody close to him could think of was tried; in substance it was very little, for there were virtually no powers of coercion in his hands. The appearance of activity, however, successfully disguised his impotence for a critical two days. Then, by the greatest of ironies, it turned out that U.S. Steel had miscalculated on what it should have been most knowledgeable about—the state of the market for steel. Just as the White House was shooting its last and noisiest bolts, the weak market forced U.S. Steel to rescind its price increases. The president was given credit for vast determination and overwhelming power; his prestige rose to new heights. He had, nevertheless, subjected his office, and the country, to grave peril.

President Eisenhower was cautious and sparing in the use of his prestige. He took great care not to spend it, even under intense provocation. Yet this policy in its way was as dangerous as President Kennedy's recklessness in the steel crisis. A dramatic illustration is Eisenhower's conduct during Senator Joseph McCarthy's attack on the Army. When Secretary of the Army Robert Stevens was subjected to humiliating treatment by the senator, a series of strong statements of support for the secretary from the president could have done much to protect him. The support was minimal, however, the president preferring to stay above the battle and protect the dignity of his office. Many concluded that, whether the president could not or merely would not expend his resources for his own subordinates, he could not be relied upon and that they, therefore, should protect themselves as best they could. This widespread conclusion resulted in a serious deterioration of the quality of government. Excessive protection of prestige can also be a mistake.

To separate out presidential prestige in this manner, however, is misleading. Although prestige is a component of power, it is really less a source than an aspect of power. The power of the president is very much like his functions. Thus, it has been fashionable to discuss individually the various roles of the president and, indeed, it is often useful to do so. Nevertheless, a president seldom can be expected to think of himself as performing now this role, now that, and now another. The roles mingle and affect one another to such a degree that they are actually indistinguishable. During the course of almost any day, he moves from meetings with his subordinates in which he deals with complex problems of organization to ceremonial functions such as dedicating monuments to welcoming ambassadors to signing bills—without break or clear transition.

Thus, the formal interview at which the president first greets a newly arrived ambassador may color the interpretive reports that that ambassador sends his government when serious matters impend. Is the president of the United States a man of great shrewdness? Can he be expected to behave with force, or will he be likely to vacillate in a crisis? Similarly, the manner and authority with which a president responds to questioning at a press conference will bear on the course of legislation before Congress, on the zeal with which officers in various departments pursue particular programs, and on the estimates that the electorate makes of him. So also with his speeches; they seldom can be expected to sway many by their sheer logic or eloquence, yet they leave a residue of impressions. Is the president devious, or is he a man of character? These questions are in the minds of most of his hearers, no matter what the subject matter of his speeches. No one speech, interview, or ceremonial act will have a decisive effect on presidential power or the course of events, but collectively all of them affect the outcome of important affairs.

If presidential conduct of even the most empty and formal details of his office is important, it does not follow that the importance consists of winning great popularity. It is quite possible to be popular simply by not giving offense. To a great extent, this was President Eisenhower's course, and in his time it had merit. Nevertheless, popularity achieved at the expense of action is usually a renunciation and a negation of power. A policy of attempting to please everyone, moreover, will probably end in pleasing no one; popularity is not the same as power and may often be incompatible with it.

Presidential popularity and power meet in the hold that the president has on his own constituency. Whenever he is able to mobilize even a substantial part of that constituency, he is a truly formidable figure. Mobilizing support at any time other than during a national crisis is extraordinarily difficult. The general public—his constituency—is normally ill informed and apathetic, even when issues of the greatest moment are at stake. Although any president can command some attention on almost any topic with which he is concerned, the task is more difficult for some presidents than for others, and the degree of support that can be obtained varies greatly. It is in just this matter of obtaining a hearing that presidential popularity and style are important. Although Franklin Roosevelt had as much popular support for his programs as any president has ever enjoyed, he nonetheless had to overcome well-entrenched opposition in Congress to many of his objectives. He accordingly inaugurated the practice of speaking directly to the public by radio. His voice was golden, and the appeal of his personality came through the static; his appeals were frequently successful. When President Kennedy encountered similar congressional opposition and was urged to use Roosevelt's "fireside chat" device, he pointed out that he had already used it as often as his predecessor. Strangely, everyone recalled the performances of FDR as having been much more frequent than in fact they had been. President Kennedy was correct, not only in his count, but in his refusal to appeal to the public by television too frequently. During his first year in office, President Johnson discovered that he was in danger of "overexposure." He curtailed his television appearances lest this particular form of political currency be hopelessly debased (and lest television audiences become too angry over the displacement of favorite programs).

Although a president can generate mass support across the nation for some particular end, he may fail to achieve that end simply because the support is weak in a particular area, say, in electing the man who happens to be chairman of a crucial congressional committee. Overwhelming support in New York and California for a presidential program may thus count for little if the president's program must be reported out by the House Interior Committee and that committee is headed by a hostile congressman from western Colorado. There may indeed be things that the president can do to move the congressman, but these will not include a direct public appeal.

Much of the time, then, the president must rely on techniques other than his ability to speak to the nation. He will have to do what other politicians (or statesmen) do: bargain and negotiate. This necessity follows particularly from the fact that political power in the United States is on the whole locally based, so that the president must deal with key congressmen and senators. Here, an intimate knowledge of the way Congress operates and of the particular needs of its individual members is extremely valuable. President Johnson probably exhibited his greatest skill here. President Kennedy, also an ex-senator, was well informed, but he lacked the long years of congressional experience and the special flair that his successor had. President Eisenhower, on the other hand, lacked the experience of either Kennedy or Johnson; in part because of this, the presidency in his time was very different from what it became under his successors. President Nixon had only indifferent success with Congress, despite his many years on Capitol Hill.

Bargaining and negotiating are the very essence of administration. In the choice of high-level bureaucrats these processes involve not only the particular agencies but senators and congressmen and interest-group leaders as well. In the conflicts among rival agencies that are such a recurrent feature of American government, the president can rarely order conflict stopped, since the issues are almost always policy matters that affect the interests of divergent groups in the general population. Often the best that a president can hope to do is to mediate, and this frequently proves futile. Sometimes a president finds himself inescapably drawn into contests between management and labor, as in the steel crisis of 1962. He may summon the parties to the White House, offer the services of government mediators, and invoke the pressure of public opinion. This aspect of the president's task is sometimes included under "the power to persuade," but simple presentation of rational arguments is seldom sufficient.

The different problems and skills involved in these various modes of politics account for the "styles" of various presidents quite as much as differences in personality. Understandably, a president such as Lyndon Johnson, who rose to prominence by his success in leading the Congress, relied on such methods when he reached the White House; just as understandably, Woodrow Wilson and John Kennedy, who both had relied on strong moral appeals to the general public, sought to make their marks by mobilizing their own large constituencies. And a president like Dwight Eisenhower, who was primarily concerned with the prestige and dignity of his office, attempted to remain apart from political conflict.

The heavy reliance on one or another of these political styles, however, may or may not be appropriate to the problems of the times. It is doubtful whether the moralism of Woodrow Wilson was the most valuable approach to the greatest problem of his time: achieving a sane international settlement after World War I. His vision of the League of Nations as a broad moral concern of the peoples of the world did leave an important legacy, which had a continuing effect in later years, but his cause might have been better served if he had counseled and bargained more intimately with the United States Senate. President Kennedy had a keen awareness of his need for congressional support, but he lacked the special talent to gain it that Lyndon Johnson brought to the presidency. By the same token, however, Johnson suffered from an inability to project to the general public a sense of moral cause. Perhaps President Eisenhower, at least in the early years of his administration, was in the happiest of circumstances in that he offered a style that met the primary need of the time. As Walter Lippmann observed, Eisenhower was a "healing president"; by simply doing little and exuding calm and dignity, he helped restore a temper of reason to a political scene that had become overheated by increasingly violent charges and countercharges.

The president's task does not permit a choice among these modes. Any president must use them all, however much his own personal proclivities incline him toward one or another. There are some occasions when a president must speak to the nation, others when he must bargain with congressmen and private citizens, and still others when he must put on a regal air. Generally, to the degree that a president seeks to influence the long-term future and bring about profound reform, he must appeal to the great constituency of the nation at large; to the degree that he seeks immediate action, he must negotiate with the power-holders of the moment; and to the degree that he seeks stability and peace, he must place himself above the tumult of the time.

As much as anything else, this is why the American presidency is nearly an impossible job: the various requirements of personality are not necessarily incompatible, but their appearance together in just the right proportions in any single individual is inevitably rare. Perhaps the best hope is that the voters will have an intuitive sense of the primary needs of the time and choose the man whose personality and training are congenial to the style appropriate to those needs.

The greatest barrier to understanding the presidency today is a widespread misconception of the character of modern government. According to this view, "government" makes decisions and chooses among clear alternatives with foreseeable results. "Decision making" has become a term in high intellectual fashion. In some respects, the emphasis on decisions has great merit; it draws attention to real events and escapes from airy abstractions that are beyond empirical testing. At its best, the approach seeks to identify all the varied participants and influences that go into the *process* of decision making.

The emphasis, however, creates an illusion of a more rational and less complex world than in fact exists. What may appear from a distance to be a "decision," that is, a deliberate choice between clearly understood alternatives made by thoughtful individuals, on closer examination may turn out to be something much more nearly approximating an accident. The participants in the "decision" may be more numerous than it appears from outside, and the considerations involved are almost invariably more complex. What actually moves the participants in the decision may not be what should have been considered; and what appear as alternative choices may on close examination not be alternatives at all. Finally, the consequences of the "decision" may be utterly different from those intended; or the consequences may be the ones intended, but they may actually result from forces very different from those invoked.

These complexities are probably easiest to see in the legislative process. Here, the number of participants is apparent, as are all the varied influences that affect the outcomes of congressional votes—the pleadings of lobbyists, constituents' letters to congressmen, the president's speeches, the chance events that appear in newspaper headlines, and so on. In the Supreme Court, which issues "decisions," the complexity of the process is also often visible. The presidency, however, is held by a single individual who gives orders that seem to be the outcome of his own personal weighing of crisply presented alternatives whose probable consequences are purportedly indicated by an efficient staff. If rationality in this sense of decision making is to be found anywhere, it should be at the apex of the government machine, the presidency.

It is true that the president makes decisions. He signs—or vetoes—bills before they become law. He chooses people to staff the chief offices of the administration. He sends messages and recommendations to Congress. Yet these are formal actions, and often these "decisions" are largely rituals. Many of the seemingly clear-cut decisions of the president, moreover, are much less clear from the White House perspective at the time they are taken. Thus, one of the most incisive choices made by a president in recent history was Kennedy's action in the Cuban missile crisis. In retrospect, it seems to have been a really dramatic turning point in modern times. The crisis appeared at the time (and still seems so) to have been a moment when mistaken action could have plunged the world into destruction. By some accounts, President Kennedy's was an incisive choice from a limited group of "options"; he made the correct one and history was transformed. Later accounts, however, indicate that the action was tentative and uncertain and that later actions were planned in a pattern of gradual escalation in a situation whose evolution was utterly unforeseeable. Much of the story is still obscure, since little is known of events and understandings in Moscow. Even in this very dramatic confrontation the retrospectively perceived pattern of crisis–decision–intended outcome is misleading; the reality through which the major participants, including the president, lived was much more complex.

This decision, like many others, recalls the battle of Borodino as described by Tolstoy in *War and Peace*: contact broken between parts of the battlefield; messages lost, delayed, or misunderstood; generals issuing irrelevant orders on the basis of mistaken understandings of the reality around them.

The genuine choices of political leaders are apt to be small ones. This is not to say that the choices are unimportant. Much that is later regarded as the result of some "great decision" is actually the consequence of a multitude of lesser decisions taken for reasons not seen as bearing on the ultimate events that they determine. To take another seemingly incisive (and as it proved, mistaken) presidential choice, consider President Truman's decision to seize the steel mills in 1952. The action was actually the outcome of a long sequence of actions and events that stretched back in time for years. These included passage of the Taft-Hartley Act in 1947, the ambiguity of a critical piece of subsequent legislation, the vague but real concession to labor leaders given by the government to persuade them to participate in the Wage Stabilization Board in 1951, the silence of the steel industry's leaders about the strength of their anger over the government's concessions to labor, the acceptance by union leaders of a presidential plea to delay a strike, and the unintended agreement of a rattled government lawyer to a suspicious judge's suggestion that the president was laying claim to "unlimited power." These incidents were components of a "decision" that was not intended until almost the moment it occurred.

Many actions by national leaders fall into this category. It is rather as though a band of travelers were headed down a road whose end they could neither see nor know. They come to a fork in the way, and arguments are propounded for one choice or the other. Ultimately one path is chosen. The party continues in the general direction it had originally intended, but perhaps the chosen fork later curves slightly; the ultimate end is changed. More important, the possibilities once offered in the choice rejected have probably been foreclosed, since on such a journey it is not usually possible to turn back and try again. Since there are many such forks and many such unwitting rejections of latent possibilities, often the great acts that seem to be the results of rational decisions are more nearly the inescapable outcomes of previous history.

The president seems to have a freer hand in foreign affairs than elsewhere. He is inevitably *the* authoritative spokesman for the United States in any confrontation with other nations. He is less often checked by political subsystems of power and influence than he is in domestic affairs. Some interest groups intervene in certain questions of foreign policy, but they are less pervasive than in other areas. The presumption of a national interest in foreign affairs, moreover, is stronger. As Theodore Lowi has shown, the American public is far more willing to support a president in foreign than in domestic affairs, even when the president's foreign policies fail disastrously. The Constitution gives Congress the power to declare war and the Senate power to pass on major diplomatic appointments and treaties, but even here a president has great advantages over Congress. By his actions he can make war very nearly inevitable, producing a situation in which Congress has no choice other than to make the formal declaration. Even this formality can be avoided. The last two major conflicts in which the United States participated, in Korea and in Vietnam, both large-scale by any test other than that of the two world wars, were fought without constitutional declarations by Congress; in a real sense, these were presidential wars.

Decisions concerning foreign affairs, however, are often more complex than they at first appear. The decision to intervene in Vietnam was one of the most fateful of recent times; it would seem a vital case of presidential decision making. Yet which president was responsible for this war? The answer is not clear. President Eisenhower refused massive military intervention to save the French when they were faced with disaster at Dien Bien Phu in 1954, but in 1955 he approved American help in training South Vietnam's army, and in 1957 Americans were wounded in Vietnam. In 1961 President Kennedy increased the number of U.S. military advisers to the South Vietnamese forces. In 1964, after American naval ships were reported attacked in the Gulf of Tonkin, President Johnson sought and got from Congress a resolution giving him authority to resist aggression in Southeast Asia; American troop strength increased to 25,000. In 1965 continuous bombing of North Vietnam began; the increase in troops accelerated. Johnson agreed to peace negotiations, but they got nowhere and the war escalated. President Nixon came into office claiming to have a secret plan to end the war but instead extended it to other parts of Indochina; the end of American military involvement in that conflict was not achieved until his second term in office.

In time it will be possible to look back and see which of these steps were the most important. Historians may be able to suggest that actions other than those taken at particular moments were possible and that *the* decision was made by a particular president; it is nevertheless probable that that president did not see matters in the historian's clear light when he made the decision.

Public opinion imposes some limitations on presidential choices in foreign affairs. Thus, in 1945 and 1946 public pressure to "bring the boys back home" and to demobilize the armed forces was irresistible, despite important diplomatic reasons for maintaining a strong force in Europe. Walter Lippmann once despairingly asserted that the public has a propensity for being wrong on the important questions of foreign policy since its opinion is always based on past situations, not the present one. Public opinion, he argued, is always against any change of policy: if the nation is at peace but becomes threatened, the public refuses to support a war; once war has been declared, the public is against making peace when the opportunity arises. This pessimistic picture is undoubtedly overdrawn. It does underline a genuine difficulty, however; much of the work of diplomacy and the management of foreign affairs must be conducted quietly and out of sight, and it is impossible for the public to be fully aware of the realities and the possibilities, including the dangers.

The enormous complexity of decision making in the White House has far-reaching implications for presidential leadership. The first of these is that the president cannot be regarded as a generalissimo issuing commands and seeing them obeyed. The problem was put bluntly in Truman's famous remark that Mr. Eisenhower, on coming to the presidency, would give orders and nothing would happen. Although the giving of orders is often part of a president's task, it is only a part and not the most essential one; indeed, it may sometimes be that when he gives orders he betrays his own failure. Beyond this, leadership in the presidency is not actually a matter of parts at all; it is more realistically the total performance of the president and his office, including his bearing in ceremonies and under stress and a host of other intangibles.

A major part of presidential leadership emerges before a time of crisis. The actions taken in a crisis, such as that involving the missiles in Cuba or the confrontation between President Kennedy and Roger Blough of U.S. Steel, undoubtedly receive greater public attention. Their success or failure, however, depends heavily on the degree to which the president has succeeded in establishing the confidence of the general public and of his own associates and subordinates; it also depends on the estimate of his character that his previous actions have created in the minds of his opponents. Thus, it is probable that President Kennedy's earlier handling of a minor issue involving Blough affected the latter's estimate of the president. In 1961 Blough was chairman of the Business Advisory Council, a body of leading businessmen that, though attached to government, was private. Secretary of Commerce Luther Hodges sought to correct certain of the council's practices that seemed questionable; the council tacitly defied Hodges and withdrew from its association with his department. President Kennedy, in an apparent effort to placate organized business, gave the council's action his blessing, but in so doing he undermined Hodges's position and opened himself to the assessment that he would give way under pressure. This background may have suggested that Kennedy would accept a fait accompli in the steel price increase. If this hypothesis is accurate, the earlier yielding helped bring on the later crisis. At the same time, however, President Kennedy had succeeded, by his general conduct of his office, in holding the various parts of government together so that in the crisis he was able to create an illusion of massively organized government power arrayed against U.S. Steel. His luck did the rest.

Similarly, in the Cuban missile crisis, Kennedy's past actions (in the confrontation with Big Steel, for example) helped form the expectation of American willingness to take drastic action, an expectation that induced Khrushchev to withdraw the missiles. But if the Soviet leader had not had an earlier very different expectation, one drawn from the impression given by Mr. Kennedy during the celebrated meeting between the two men in Vienna, perhaps the rash Soviet attempt to place the missiles in Cuba would never have been made in the first place. Too intense a preoccupation with this sort of consideration on the part of a president and his advisers, however, can lead to disaster, as with the fateful "domino theory" applied to Vietnam.

If the president's problems are as large and diffuse as these events suggest, the personal characteristics he need bring to the office are exceedingly difficult to define. It is easy to say that he should have charisma, the God-given quality of the "born leader." About this, however, there is little to say other than to name it and to note that it is a quality that has been possessed by surprisingly few American presidents. Among modern presidents, it will probably be agreed that Franklin and Theodore Roosevelt were natural leaders. In the presence of his still proliferating myth, President Kennedy remains a question on this score; it is nevertheless possible that he in fact lacked the quality. There are no others among twentieth-century presidents, and a few among their predecessors, who could be labeled charismatic, yet they included many highly successful leaders.

If the gifted natural leader behind whom men will instinctively fall in line has been rare among American presidents, the reasons lie deep in American character and American politics. Americans have generally distrusted men strikingly endowed with the "charismatic" quality. The egalitarian spirit of American life noted by observers of the United States from Tocqueville on sooner or later produces a widespread inclination to diminish the stature and reputation of any man who becomes eminent. Adulation of leaders does occur, but it happens most commonly and most strongly after they are dead. Beyond this, the political institutions of the nation place many barriers in the way of anyone who might remotely suggest a man on horseback. Power to operate through these institutions must surmount innumerable local and functional obstacles not easily overcome without negotiation and payment of tribute; to brush them aside would require a mass movement of dimensions and intensity unlike anything seen in America.

The inborn qualities that make for success in presidential leadership are thus rather different from those that first come to mind at the mention of "natural" leadership. The most obvious quality needed is the highly intuitive capacity to sense the state of public feeling—to assess the extent and the intensity of satisfaction or dissatisfaction and even *potential* pleasure or displeasure of the nation as a whole and as a collection of factions. Experience, study, and training undoubtedly deepen this capacity, but ultimately it is a natural gift that a successful president must have. Whatever the resources of attitude and opinion surveys placed at his disposal, the president must test them by his own intuition and interpret them. This is not to say that presidential leadership is a trick by which a president, having sensed the state of the public mind, scurries to assume a position perfectly attuned with it. He must make his assessment of existing opinion, but he must also lead. Franklin Roosevelt gave a splendid example of what is involved when he made his famous Quarantine Speech in 1937 warning of the Nazi danger. He was clearly ahead of public opinion, and he quickly realized that he was in danger of becoming isolated in the van. He retreated—but only sufficiently to renew contact with those he had to lead.

The ability to negotiate and bargain among significant and coherent segments of the political public is also related to inborn traits of personality. This ability is shared by many individuals who have no potential for leadership; but the charm, the cool-headedness, and other qualities that yield success in mediation—or even in selling—are highly useful in the higgling that goes on in the political marketplace, a process from which no president who wishes to influence the course of things can be aloof. Perhaps to say this is to degrade the concept of leadership to something less exalted than many would wish. Nevertheless, even when the process is scorned as so much "wheeling and dealing," the results obtained are frequently as acceptable as those won by more glorious battles.

Usually there is also something intensely personal, whether inborn or not, in the capacity to manage a complex organization. Obviously, the talent for administration may be cultivated and improved. Some presidents, Franklin Roosevelt for example, had neither talent nor taste in this direction. Others, Herbert Hoover most notably, had both the talent and the taste. The ability is certainly valuable in a president, but, as the examples suggest, it is far less important than other qualities. It almost seems that purely organizational ability conflicts with political ability and that, to the degree that a president devotes himself to administrative tidiness, he falls short in the more fundamental aspects of his task. Perhaps this underlines the observation that a president must be first of all a politician if he is to be a leader.

The trait that may ultimately be the most crucial in a president is a sense for power. He must have an almost instinctive understanding of the sources of power, its locations, and how it may be grasped. Usually this implies that he has a taste for power, although that is not a requirement or even an invariable accompaniment of the sense. It is nevertheless essential that a president give unremitting attention to the implications for his power of his every act and, indeed, of virtually everything that happens. It is a paradox that, if a president consistently conserves and protects his power, he will less frequently be compelled to resort to its overt invocation and application. To cite a famous example, during 1957 President Eisenhower found himself in a situation in which he had no choice but to send a military force into Little Rock, Arkansas, after he had created the incorrect impression that he would not act decisively if school integration were opposed. The weakness he seemed to betray became a reality in that greater force than he or anyone else desired became necessary. Had he been willing to state firmly that he would see that the law would be enforced, it is probable, paradoxically, that he would not have had to resort to the action he took. Power is greatest and most successful when its overt employment is unnecessary. To achieve this condition, however, a president must always look to the future and to the consequences of his actions. The prospect of a diminution of his power in future crises was, more than anything else, the main reason for the explosiveness of President Kennedy's reaction to the unexpected announcement of U.S. Steel that its prices were being increased.

However obvious it may be, it is worth asserting that high intelligence is a primary need in the presidency. Perhaps not everyone would agree that all American presidents have possessed this attribute, yet most have. Only a few have been men of high culture. But culture is not the same as intelligence, and it is more important for a president to possess the common touch than to be at home among the great works of art and literature. Nevertheless, he must be able to gain the services of intellectuals and use their advice. (The alienation of the intellectual community from the Republican party since the early Eisenhower years will prove a continuing handicap to the Republican presidents unless it can be countered.) The capacity to grasp the essentials of complex matters, however, is the indispensable intellectual trait of a modern president. When he must decide on costly weapon systems complicated beyond the understanding of any but trained imaginations, when he must weigh the relative costs (political as well as economic) of inflation or a seriously adverse balance of payments against high unemployment, when he must assess the chances for a negotiated peace at a time when a substantial public is rigidly committed to complete victory—when he must do these and many other things concurrently and then mobilize support for his choices, it is obvious that the intellectual demands of his job are hardly less than superhuman.

Vital as these components of presidential leadership are, however, they pale beside an intangible that is virtually immune to analysis—character. In the harsh light of publicity that envelops the presidency, few defects can remain invisible for long. The false and the insincere are ultimately apt to be detected by even the humblest watcher on television. It may not occur immediately, but so often are the behavior and the person of the president placed before the public that dissimulation and disguise cannot long escape detection. Incidents such as the Watergate scandal in the Nixon administration ultimately diminish the presidency and damage the nation. Few men who reach the presidency can expect to be loved or even liked; fortunately, this is not required. What is essential is that at crucial moments the president be trusted. Every president must renew his powers often, sometimes each day. What those powers are depends to a large degree on the quality of presidential leadership. If that leadership is debased by deceit or the contriving of a crisis, the popular support gained thereby may wither as quickly and completely as it flowered.

The Presidency in the
Political Order

chapter six

One of the most difficult problems in understanding political reality is in comprehending the relation between the formal and the informal aspects of the system. Indeed, it is easy to draw two separate and entirely different pictures—and to label one false and the other true. To do this, however, is to make a mistake. The formal rules set forth in the Constitution and their interpretation by the Supreme Court are hard realities to which practice must conform. The manner of conforming, nevertheless, is often different from anything foreseen by the founders or deducible from the legal documents. The American political order, moreover, although one of the most stable of modern times, is subject to continual change. An accurate description for one era may be quite misleading if applied to another. An account of the political order must be founded on a sense of where it is heading as well as where it has been. The fashionable contrast between modern and traditional societies is never polar; even the traditional societies change, and modern societies—of which the United States is the prime example—have their strong and persistent traditions.

The political system of the United States institutionalizes a variety of values, some of them at odds with each other. An emphasis upon one aspect of the order stresses certain values—but is open to a challenge based upon a preference for other values. Nevertheless, some values are higher in the general scale of preferences held by the nation at large, and these preferences ultimately test the system and its parts. Evaluation of a particular institution is not merely a matter of taste.

The formal definition of the presidency has changed markedly over time and can be expected to change more, even from incumbent to incumbent. And it has often embodied values different from those championed by Congress. This definition of the presidency cannot help being caught up in the major currents that sweep American society, though it, in turn, has enormous capacities for directing those currents. To ask what is to become of the presidency is to ask what is to become of the entire American political order.

Americans persistently perceive their government in the terms chosen by the framers of the Constitution. This is fortunate, since the pervasive spirit of the framers' outlook carried an emphasis upon liberty. The American reverence for the framers and their work has nevertheless kept alive a vision of politics in the United States that becomes more and more unrealistic with each passing year. Constitutional origins and tradition both dwell upon federalism and the separation of powers. Both doctrines are undeniably woven into the entire system. The difficulty we encounter with them is that neither has had a constant meaning.

The traditional vision is that, under federalism, government in the United States consists of distinct state and national levels, each with its own peculiar powers and sources of authority. These two levels of government occasionally conflict with each other, raising problems of what each considers to be properly its own. The rest of the time, however, the two go their separate ways, performing their separate and characteristic functions. Observations that reality is not quite like this tend to be framed as warnings that corruption or usurpation is taking place, that the federal government is growing strong at the expense of the states.

It is doubtful whether such a vision was ever satisfactory. Shortly after the new government was launched, cries arose that the Constitution was being perverted. Indeed, the cries sometimes had a foundation that many of their present counterparts lack. Today, however, the picture is not only grossly inaccurate; it is a travesty upon the flexibility of the Constitution drawn in 1787.

Federalism in the twentieth century is an intricate pattern of shared functions, the states and the federal government being enmeshed with each other at the inception, the planning, and the execution of many policies. Repeatedly the "central government" is found responding to the initiatives of local governments— themselves formally creatures of the state governments—and providing money to the states to be spent by the local units. The process is described nowhere in the Constitution, yet it is thoroughly constitutional. Again and again, the supposedly insulated levels of government work together so intimately and cooperatively that there seems to be a single coherent system. Yet just as it begins to appear that this, rather than the traditional vision of opposing levels, is the essential picture, crises involving states' rights and civil rights arise, and it is apparent that reality is mixed. The truth is that the states have neither been absorbed by nor have they absorbed the federal government and that important frictions remain within a system still constantly changing.

Similarly, the traditional vision holds with regard to the separation of powers. In this vision the three coordinate branches of the federal government, like the two levels, occasionally clash, but for the most part they also go their separate ways playing their allotted roles. Although the conflicts provide drama and receive much attention, the important political reality is the collaboration between the executive and the legislative branches. There are serious conflicts in the making of policy; much of politics has to do with conflict, but many of the most important conflicts occur in both branches. The typical pattern, indeed, is one in which some members of the executive and some members of Congress are aligned against other members of the executive and other members of Congress, each side with its supporters in private interest groups and local elites. But so far as the two branches themselves are concerned, the important fact is mutual dependency. Congress is probably increasingly incapable of formulating policy on most of the matters on which it must take formal action. It may alter and criticize proposals before it; often it must mediate the final stages of conflict aroused by the proposals; but only rarely can it successfully introduce and effectuate a major change of policy by its own unaided initiative.

To understand the presidency, it is necessary, then, to look upon the whole system. In particular, it is essential to consider the central problems that the system has had to solve. The first of these is easy to ignore, for it has been solved brilliantly in America. It is, very simply, the problem of unity, of maintaining a single nation. The problem was implicit in the motivation of the remarkable band of men who engineered a virtual coup d'état in discarding the Articles of Confederation and substituting the Constitution. It was an issue that smoldered below the surface until 1860, when it brought civil war. Since then, we have tended to take as thoroughly settled the view that there should be a single nation stretching across a continental expanse and encompassing millions of people from different races, religions, and cultures.

Mere national survival, however, has never been the whole of the American political problem. Survival has always been taken to mean something considerably more, the persistence of values for which the overworked words *equality* and *liberty* are still the only terms to use. The nation might have continued in being without the ordeal of civil war if the North had been willing to acquiesce in the extension of slavery to the West. To achieve the aims of liberty and equality concurrently with unity has been enormously difficult.

Federalism has probably been the single most important political device by which the nation has been preserved. This basic compromise has made many others possible. The irony here is that the compromise was between the various states on the one hand and the nation on the other, not the most important issue of American history. In a larger sense, however, federalism from the start has been a compromise between the nation and its parts, the parts being not states but less formal units, local and functional elites. Federalism has been the means by which the power held by these groups has been recognized and accepted in return for their acceptance and support of the nation. The fundamental principle underlying this compromise—seen with some clarity by James Madison when the Constitution was formulated—is that small units, being usually less diverse than large ones, are more likely to encourage the structuring of power relationships and the formation of stable elites. Thus, state units have not only preserved the power of local elites and interest groups, but they have also been the channel for additional resources to flow from the nation to the local units. The nation in return has enjoyed the benefits of the organization and the disciplining of elements of the population that might otherwise have gone their separate ways or been disruptive.

The presidency has probably been essential to the success of federalism in the United States. It is possible to imagine a United States existing within the framework of the Articles of Confederation, but the absence of a central executive would have condemned such a nation to a much lesser stature. Besides other deficiencies, it would have had a poorer economy and less capacity to defend itself. The character of the executive has been almost as important as the fact of an executive's existence. There was a genuine possibility that a plural or a collegial executive might have been chosen by the constitutional founders. Although such an executive might have worked, the nation would not likely have been as cohesive. It would have been without an important symbol: even a modern people must have ceremony and ritual if they are to endure the ordeals that accompany life in common. More important, however, the nation would have sacrificed incisive leadership at critical junctures. If a collegial executive had been adopted by the framers, it might have been chosen either in Congress or directly by the electorate. Either way would probably have resulted in divided leadership in time of crisis. Britain, indeed, has selected her national leaders from Parliament and has been very successful, but she is far less diverse than the United States and in recent times has relied upon party machinery to elevate the leaders above Parliament.

The presidency, in representing the national aspect of political life, has been important to the evolution of federalism; the office has been the medium for reasserting national values. These values include not only elementary national survival and unity but liberty and equality, which lie at the heart of the American ethos. Repeatedly, the presidency has, of necessity, been the focus of efforts on behalf of weak minorities and the underprivileged; in recent years it has shared this burden with the Supreme Court. Most of the government initiative to end racial segregation has come from the president and from the Court. When the Supreme Court decided in 1954 that segregated education was contrary to the "equal protection of the laws" clause of the Fourteenth Amendment, it started a long chain of events. Though state and local governments and individual congressmen could and did resist desegregation, the president and the federal executive were compelled to align themselves with the Court. Even President Eisenhower, who strongly believed in the sanctity of state and local autonomy, responded to defiance in Arkansas with military force.

The reason for the alignment of the Supreme Court and the presidency is that both have the same constituency, the whole nation. Both are responsible to *all* the people, and neither is susceptible to the pressures of the local holders of power to the degree that congressmen and state officials are. This is not to say that either the president or the Court can always be relied upon to defend the rights and interests of the weak, merely that they are better able, and hence more likely, to do so. Nor can it be assumed that the president and the Supreme Court will always take the same view of every controversy. There are different ways of regarding the interests of the weak, and not all issues involve such interests. Thus, in the *Youngstown* decision of 1952, the Court resoundingly denied presidential power to seize the steel mills. Moreover, the Court very nearly demolished Franklin Roosevelt's New Deal in a series of adverse decisions. On the whole, however, the Court has been reluctant to oppose presidential power. The outcome of its demolition activities in the 1930s included the abortive "court packing" incident and then a reversal of the Court's attitude toward New Deal activism; from 1936 on, the Court tended to accept programs under legislation sponsored by the president. The hostility of the Supreme Court to presidential programs in the early 1930s is not likely to be repeated. Some differences and even clashes between the presidency and the Court will occur, but no persistent pattern of hostility is probable.

In contrast to the presidency (and the Supreme Court), the states are necessarily narrow in outlook and have no forum other than Congress in which anything approaching a view of the nation as a whole is possible. And Congress, being an assembly of the representatives of relatively small constituencies, is only occasionally able to rise above the context of the contending claims of these constituencies. Certainly many individual senators and congressmen are individuals of broad vision, but they have to keep in mind the nature of their own constituencies. Often, we like to assume that, since all localities of the nation are represented in Congress, all values cherished by the American people are likewise fully represented and that, in aggregate, Congress represents the nation as well as the president does. This assumption, however, is not justified; many values and interests are underrepresented or not represented at all in Congress: the interests of the poor and the weak, nonmaterial and noneconomic values especially. In Congress, policy tends to be settled by logrolling, that is, mutual exchange of support among the representatives of different constituencies for their own enterprises, with the result that the interests of groups lacking substantial bases of power in the localities are ignored. Just because the president is not selected on this basis and because his responsibility is to all the people, he is able to include in the policies he supports a greater range of interests. As a consequence, his policies are more likely to embrace the interests of those who have been left out of the pattern of congressional initiative. The evidence is abundant that, if innovations of policy in favor of the poor, the blacks and Chicanos, the impotent minorities of all kinds are to be made, the initiative has to come not only from the executive branch of the federal government but from the presidency itself. Only the president has the resources of power to act on their behalf, and only he has a constituency constructed so as to include them in the effective scheme of power.

The relationship of the presidency to the basic value of liberty is more complex, but the same set of considerations applies. Since the presidency is the point on which the greatest diversity of pressures comes to bear, here the checking of organized power by organized power that Madison noted as the great advantage of a large constituency is at a maximum in the American system. This advantage largely accounts for the ability of the president to initiate programs for groups at the lower end of the social spectrum. The most vivid modern illustration of this principle in operation involves civil rights. Political power in Mississippi has long been concentrated in white hands. Thus, giving authority over civil rights to the counties of that state or to its governor (or deferring to the state's representatives in Congress) necessarily resulted in perpetuation of the local system in which the rights of blacks were often ignored. The defense of the rights of blacks in Mississippi, thus, almost necessarily had to lie with the federal government and in its executive. In short, the leadership had to come from the presidency.

As the opposition of states' rights and civil rights in this illustration suggests, the claim of the states to be free of interference is an issue of liberty also. And here the matter becomes very complicated indeed. Whose liberty is to be protected? If the federal government intervenes in Mississippi, is there not an infringement of freedom? This question inevitably becomes entangled with questions on the meaning of self-government. If the states are taken as concrete entities, then the significant conclusion is that federal intervention on behalf of blacks is interference with the freedom of the states. If the states are not regarded as such concrete entities, however, the conclusion is very different. The conflict then appears as one between different sets of human individuals. It is in this latter light that the presidency must be seen as a defender of freedom. Quite understandably, though, those groups that have benefited from local systems of unequally distributed power will not so regard it.

A strong tradition of mistrust for the presidency has always existed, and it has always been related to fear of tyranny. This mistrust, in some respects a healthy one, is a compound of rather different fears. One of these has been essentially a fear of loss of state autonomy to a supposedly grasping central authority. This, in turn, is related to the less publicized but probably more keenly felt fear that expanded presidential power might undermine the power systems of interest group elites that thrive on a pattern of government decentralization. The most lurid fear, however, is that the president might gather all the threads of power into his hands and establish himself as a dictator. From the early days of the republic down to the time of Andrew Jackson, this was expressed as fear of a reestablished monarchy. And except for the language, essentially the same charges were directed against Lyndon Johnson and Richard Nixon. How far does the justification for this persistent fear reach?

The strongest part of any such justification lies in the president's powers in military and foreign affairs. It was because of these powers that the French critic Riencourt painted his alarming picture of the coming Caesars, the Caesars in question being future American presidents. In an immediate and genuinely alarming sense, the powers of the president in time of war are great. As commander in chief, he can act with seemingly few limitations. That during the last wars in which the United States has engaged the infringements upon liberty made in the president's name have been relatively moderate in no way mitigates the danger that exists. The vagueness of the constitutional authority of the president suggests that the possibilities of presidential action in crisis may not yet have been fully exploited. And it is worth recalling that some of the actions that have been taken have been very strong indeed. The shameful arbitrary infringements of the rights of Japanese-Americans during World War II should not be forgotten.

It is doubtful, however, that the threats to liberty that in wartime may be made by the president or in his name are possible simply because presidential authority is vaguely defined in the Constitution. Probably the most serious invasions of individual rights by presidential action came from Lincoln. Some of his actions were indeed found to be beyond his constitutional powers, but only after the crisis had passed. Supreme Court review of the somber questions related to the Japanese-American evacuation also took years. The unfortunate fact seems to be that, during wartime crises, constitutional limitations are brushed aside, and little recourse for the injured is possible so long as the crisis lasts. Moreover, it is also doubtful that presidential authority is often the sole ground for arbitrary actions. Given a sufficient crisis— and war is almost invariably sufficient—Congress is usually willing to pass measures giving a color of legality to almost anything the president and his military advisers urge as necessary. There is little evidence to justify a belief that Congress is a better guardian of individual liberties in wartime than the president, or that any formally stated constitutional provisions could prevent future outrages of the sort we have already seen. The principle at work here seems to be *inter arma silent leges.*

Such dangers to liberty are closely related to the dangers arising from the tendencies toward autonomy of important segments of the sprawling bureaucratic structure. Thus, the military establishment, reasoning from its own technical perspective, is often able to press successfully for measures that prove disastrous because of the partial nature of that perspective. The record of violence loosed upon the population of Indochina, violence far out of proportion to the ends conceivably to be attained, is likely to stand in history as a reproach to the nation— and to the presidents who agreed to it. And yet, it is doubtful whether Congress or any other institution could have withstood the pressures for that course of action.

The threat posed by the Nixon presidency evoked a variety of fears. One was corruption, the exchange of governmental favors for money. Another was the invasion of the rights and privacy of citizens. And perhaps the largest was the attempt to centralize power in White House hands. All were based in some sense on reality. The danger in the attempt to build power in the White House, however, derived less from the intended centralization than from the means adopted. These consisted, not of compromise and accommodation, but of simple orders and commands over elements of government administration. Attempts to coordinate different aspects of policy and to make government responsive to the constituency of the entire nation are legitimate and necessary. What happened in the early 1970s, however, was that the system of presidential responsibility was subverted and an attempt was made to substitute a pattern of personal presidential authority for democratic consent obtained through the many patterns of consultation that have developed during the 200 years of the Republic. In the end, the prospect of impeachment gave the coup de grace to the attempt, but it was probably doomed before that prospect became a certainty. The recourse of impeachment was important, but the existence of an organized opposition, an alert and suspicious press an independent judiciary, and a rival center of power in the Congress were the essential means of defense. They proved formidable indeed.

The really persistent, and frightening, fact about the modern presidency is that while the office has increasingly become a primary medium for responsible government in the United States, the president does not control the government in either the making or the administering of policy. It is difficult to foresee any president having such control. The United States is too large, too diverse, and too rapidly changing for firm control from the White House ever to be possible. Moreover, the remarkable system of devolution of the work of government to separate systems of governance, in each of which interest groups, local elites, congressmen, and other public representatives assume autonomous control over particular areas of public policy, is so strongly established that nothing is likely to produce any radical change in the American ways of government in a short time.

The resulting fragmentation of American policy has nevertheless conferred real benefits on the nation. The primary benefit is that power-holding groups have been induced, by their co-optation into many subsystems of government, to acquiesce in the continuation of the United States as a nation and have concurrently demonstrated a willingness to accept a minimum number of national objectives and national policies. The tradition of leaving many public policies to be carried out by the states, localities, and even private associations, whether through grants-in-aid, schemes of "consultation," or the creation of autonomous administrative bodies, has resulted in stability where a more rigid and a more centralized system might long ago have broken apart. Every man who has reached the presidency has had at least an intuitive appreciation of these benefits.

In accepting the power and the participation of these many political subsystems, however, a president accepts strong limitations upon his own power—and upon the obligations he has to those of his constituents not fortunate enough to be included within any of the subsystems that are co-opted. Each time the president "consults" with a major farm organization about his choice for secretary of agriculture, every time he chooses a major corporation executive to head the Department of Defense or a leading banker to be secretary of the treasury, he yields up a significant part of his ability to affect the policies controlled by those departments. In these and many other ways, he concedes that he must have the support of power-holding elements in the nation. And he has little other choice than to act in this manner. At best, he may cut to a minimum the concessions that he is obliged to make.

By thus insuring at least a minimum of national unity and domestic peace, however, a president repudiates a substantial part of the obligation under which he was elected. This cruel dilemma is almost never explicitly acknowledged. The folklore of American politics, with its glorification of decentralization and deep fear of dictatorship and of government in general, makes possible the presentation of the concessions as themselves a form of democracy. The deference to power-holding groups thus appears as democratic self-determination and the avoidance of compulsion (which is conveniently left to the autonomous subsystems).

The president, nonetheless, remains in office as the elected representative of *all* the people. He must speak and act for those individuals outside the effective schemes of representation and power built upon the fragmented pattern of representation in Congress and the states. He must also see the demands of the many elements of the population in relation to each other and to the needs of the nation as a whole, and if he does not take a view that includes the powerless as well as the powerful, the national interest as well as the particular interests, there is nobody else who can.

In the past the nation was geographically much larger in relation to its population than it is now; with poor communications the nation could realistically be regarded as a collection of separate parts. The economy was much less integrated, and America's place in the world allowed it the luxury of safe isolation. Inevitably, modern conditions have vastly expanded the obligations of the presidency. Foreign policy cannot be left to the play of contending domestic factions without serious danger. The educational needs of the nation cannot be simply declared a matter for localities to pay for or to decide. Natural resources cannot be given over to exploitative interests to do with as they will. So it is in many areas. The federal government again and again is compelled, by the rising demands from hitherto powerless groups and by dangers visible from a national perspective, to take new kinds of action. The federal government, however, is still highly fragmented and subject to the power of elites of various kinds. Thus, here again, the needs can be met only if the responsibility is accepted in the White House.

If the responsibility of the presidency is large and growing, the power of the office is often inadequate. One of the greatest dangers to American democracy is that the gap between the power and the responsibility of the presidency may widen. To the degree that the two are disproportionate, the nation will be in danger from foreign threats and domestic disorder. To the degree that the president is unable to meet his obligations, demands for justice by deprived minorities will go unsatisfied and the quality of life in many ways will be poorer than it might be. The obligation of the president in the largest terms is to mobilize political power and direct it toward the ends of social justice and national security. But in the existing American context presidential power is limited.

For this reason, any president has to be continually concerned with the capacities of his office. He is endowed at election with the aura that goes to the chief of state of the most powerful nation of the world. He receives adulation on a scale known to few other men. He bears the powers acknowledged as his under the Constitution and in many legislative acts. He is head of the armed forces and the entire executive branch. He is head of his party. And yet the power that he can assume from these sources is often insufficient and, indeed, sometimes illusory. Like a general, he has continually to choose among the possible battles he might join, avoiding some and engaging in others. He must build his power for the contests he cannot avoid.

The presidency is not and never can be a machine that runs itself or continues in operation untended. Though the vastly increased demands upon the office have brought about a large increase in the scope of the Executive Office of the President, routinization of the presidency has not been achieved. This is not because the workload of the office, great though it is, is too vast to be encompassed by competent organization. It has been suggested more than once that the crushing load upon the president should be divided among a number of people—assistant presidents or a cabinet of vice-presidents. While undoubtedly some presidential chores could be well done by assistants, most of the work of the presidency cannot be divided or given over to others, whatever their titles, without a radical and probably dangerous change in the system of responsibility. If the assistant presidents were chosen by the president himself and received their commissions directly from him, the situation would hardly be different from the present one, in which a sizable number of assistants are already available to the president. If, on the other hand, the assistant presidents were chosen by election or by Congress—or by any method that gave them authority in any degree independent of the president—the way would be open to a further division of responsibility in a political system already too fragmented. The president's burden may be heavy, but he must carry it.

In an age of bureaucracy, the presidency remains a remarkably personal office. The individual who occupies it makes a difference; at almost any time it can be said that, had someone else been chosen to the office, things would have been different. At fateful moments, choices appropriate only to a deity fall upon the president, a mortal. At such moments, the president needs all the knowledge his staff can give him; he needs all the wit and shrewdness his years of political experience can provide; he needs skepticism in the face of ready-made advice; and he needs ingenuity enough to perceive possibilities that have not been mentioned to him. But most of all he needs—and the nation needs in him—a quality of humanity, the sense that the vast power momentarily his to command is the power to devastate the earth and destroy life. His character and wisdom in these moments are the critical elements in any action he invokes. And here, unfortunately, there are no guarantees.

Without question, there are genuine dangers in our dependence on this office and on a single man. While some of these dangers consist of the possibility that a president may abuse his power, others are that he will not use his power wisely or that he will not use it at all when it is needed. For better or worse, a president must be a leader—a national leader. His power will depend less on the terms of the Constitution or of legislation than on how well he is able to articulate the aspirations of the American people and apply them to national problems. This may involve him at one moment in bitter struggle for the passage of some reform or even in leading the conduct of a great war. But at another moment it may require that he give voice to the nation's great sorrow, as Lincoln did at Gettysburg. Ultimately, like Lincoln, he must become the medium of national reconciliation and must rededicate the nation toward its own best ends.

The Presidents

George Washington	1789–1797
John Adams	1797–1801
Thomas Jefferson	1801–1809
James Madison	1809–1817
James Monroe	1817–1825
John Quincy Adams	1825–1829
Andrew Jackson	1829–1837
Martin Van Buren	1837–1841
William Henry Harrison	1841
John Tyler	1841–1845
James K. Polk	1845–1849
Zachary Taylor	1849–1850
Millard Fillmore	1850–1853
Franklin Pierce	1853–1857
James Buchanan	1857–1861
Abraham Lincoln	1861–1865
Andrew Johnson	1865–1869
Ulysses S. Grant	1869–1877
Rutherford B. Hayes	1877–1881
James A. Garfield	1881
Chester A. Arthur	1881–1885
Grover Cleveland	1885–1889
Benjamin Harrison	1889–1893

Grover Cleveland	1893–1897
William McKinley	1897–1901
Theodore Roosevelt	1901–1909
William Howard Taft	1909–1913
Woodrow Wilson	1913–1921
Warren G. Harding	1921–1923
Calvin Coolidge	1923–1929
Herbert Hoover	1929–1933
Franklin Delano Roosevelt	1933–1945
Harry S Truman	1945–1953
Dwight D. Eisenhower	1953–1961
John F. Kennedy	1961–1963
Lyndon B. Johnson	1963–1969
Richard M. Nixon	1969–1974
Gerald R. Ford	1974–

The Constitution on the Presidency

ARTICLE II

Section 1. 1. The executive power shall be vested in a President of the United States of America. He shall hold his office during the term of four years, and, together with the Vice-President, chosen for the same term, be elected as follows:

2. Each state shall appoint, in such manner as the legislature thereof may direct, a number of electors, equal to the whole number of Senators and Representatives to which the State may be entitled in the Congress; but no Senator or Representative, or person holding an office of trust or profit under the United States, shall be appointed an elector.

3.* The electors shall meet in their respective states and vote by ballot for two persons, of whom one at least shall not be an inhabitant of the same state with themselves. And they shall make a list of all the persons voted for, and of the number of votes for each; which list they shall sign and certify, and transmit sealed to the seat of the government of the United States, directed to the President of the Senate. The President of the Senate shall, in the presence of the Senate and House of Representatives, open all the certificates, and the votes shall then be counted. The person having the greatest number of votes shall be the President, if such a number a majority of the whole number of electors appointed; and if there be more than one who have such majority, and have an equal number of votes, then the House of Representatives shall immediately choose by ballot one of them for President; and if no person have a

---

*This paragraph was superseded by the Twelfth Amendment.

majority, then from the five highest on the list the said House shall in like manner choose the President. But in choosing the President the votes shall be taken by states, the representation from each state having one vote; a quorum for this purpose shall consist of a member or members from two-thirds of the states, and a majority of all the states shall be necessary to a choice. In every case, after the choice of the President, the person having the greatest number of votes of the electors shall be the Vice-President. But if there should remain two or more who have equal votes, the Senate shall choose from them by ballot the Vice-President.

4. The Congress may determine the time of choosing the electors and the day on which they shall give their votes, which day shall be the same throughout the United States.

5. No person except a natural born citizen, or a citizen of the United States, at the time of the adoption of this Constitution, shall be eligible to the office of President; neither shall any person be eligible to that office who shall not have attained to the age of thirty-five years, and been fourteen years a resident within the United States.

6. In case of the removal of the President from office, or of his death, resignation, or inability to discharge the powers and duties of the said office, the same shall devolve on the Vice-President, and the Congress may by law provide for the case of removal, death, resignation, or inability, both of the President and Vice-President, declaring what officer shall then act as President, and such officer shall act accordingly until the disability be removed or a President shall be elected.

7. The President shall, at stated times, receive for his services a compensation, which shall neither be increased nor diminished during the period for which he shall have been elected, and he shall not receive within that period any other emolument from the United States or any of them.

8. Before he enter on the execution of his office he shall take the following oath or affirmation:

> I do solemnly swear (or affirm) that I will faithfully execute the office of President of the United States, and will to the best of my ability preserve, protect, and defend the Constitution of the United States.

Section 2. 1. The President shall be Commander-in-Chief of the Army and Navy of the United States, and of the militia of the several states when called into the actual service of the United States; he may require the opinion, in writing, of the principal officer in each of the executive departments, upon any subject relating to the duties of their respective offices, and he shall have power to grant reprieves and pardons for offenses against the United States, except in cases of impeachment.

2. He shall have power, by and with the advice and consent of the Senate, to make treaties, provided two-thirds of the Senators present concur; and he shall nominate, and, by and with the advice and consent of the Senate, shall appoint ambassadors, other public ministers and consuls, judges of the Supreme Court, and all other officers of the United States, whose appointments are not herein otherwise provided for, and which shall be established by law; but the Congress may by law vest the appointment of such inferior officers, as they think proper, in the President alone, in the courts of law, or in the heads of departments.

3. The President shall have power to fill up all vacancies that may happen during the recess of the Senate, by granting commissions which shall expire at the end of their next session.

Section 3. He shall from time to time give to the Congress information of the state of the union, and recommend to their consideration such measures as he shall judge necessary and expedient; he may, on extraordinary occasions, convene both houses, or either of them, and in case of disagreement between them with respect to the time of adjournment, he may adjourn them to such time as he shall think proper; he shall receive ambassadors and other public ministers; he shall take care that the laws be faithfully executed, and shall commission all the officers of the United States.

Section 4. The President, Vice-President, and all civil officers of the United States shall be removed from office on impeachment for and conviction of treason, bribery, or other high crimes and misdemeanors.

OTHER PROVISIONS

ARTICLE I

Section 3. 6. The Senate shall have the sole power to try all impeachments. When sitting for that purpose, they shall be on oath or affirmation. When the President of the United States is tried, the Chief Justice shall preside; and no person shall be convicted without the concurrence of two-thirds of the members present.

Section 7. 2. Every bill which shall have passed the House of Representatives and the Senate shall, before it becomes a law, be presented to the President of the United States; if he approve he shall sign it, but if not he shall return it, with his objections to that house in which it shall have originated, who shall enter the objections at large on their journal and proceed to reconsider it. If after such reconsideration two-thirds of that house shall agree to pass the bill, it shall be sent, together with the objections, to the other house, by which it shall likewise be reconsidered, and if approved by two-thirds of that house it shall become a law. But in all such cases the votes of both houses shall be determined by yeas and nays, the names of the persons voting for and against the bill shall be entered on the journal of each house respectively. If any bill shall not be returned by the President within ten days (Sundays excepted) after it shall have been presented to him, the same shall be a law, in like manner as if he had signed it unless the Congress by their adjournment prevent its return, in which case it shall not be a law.

3. Every order, resolution, or vote to which the concurrence of the Senate and House of Representatives may be necessary (except on a question of adjournment) shall be presented to the President of the United States; and before the same shall take effect, shall be approved by him, or being disapproved by him, shall be repassed by two-thirds of the Senate and House of Representatives, according to the rules and limitations prescribed in the case of a bill.

Amendment XII

The electors shall meet in their respective states and vote by ballot for President and Vice-President, one of whom, at least, shall not be an inhabitant of the same state with themselves; they shall name in their ballots the person voted for as President, and in distinct ballots the person voted for as Vice-President, and they shall make distinct lists of all persons voted for as President and of all persons voted for as Vice-President, and of the number of votes for each; which lists they shall sign and certify, and transmit sealed to the seat of the government of the United States, directed to the President of the Senate. The President of the Senate shall, in the presence of the Senate and House of Representatives, open all the certificates and the votes shall then be counted. The person having the greatest number of votes for President shall be the President, if such number be a majority of the whole number of electors appointed; and if no person have such majority, then from the persons having the highest numbers not exceeding three on the list of those voted for as President, the House of Representatives shall choose immediately, by ballot, the President. But in choosing the President the votes shall be taken by states, the representation from each state having one vote; a quorum for this purpose shall consist of a member or members from two-thirds of the states, and a majority of all the states shall be necessary to a choice. And if the House of Representatives shall not choose a President whenever the right of choice shall devolve upon them, before the fourth day of March next following, then the Vice-President shall act as President, as in the case of the death or other constitutional disability of the President.

The person having the greatest number of votes as Vice-President shall be the Vice-President, if such number be a majority of the whole number of electors appointed; and if no person have a majority, then from the two highest numbers on the list the Senate shall choose the Vice-President; a quorum for the purpose shall consist of two-thirds of the whole number of Senators, and a majority of the whole number shall be necessary to a choice. But no person constitutionally ineligible to the office of President shall be eligible to that of Vice-President of the United States.

AMENDMENT XX

Section 1. The terms of the President and Vice-President shall end at noon on the 20th day of January, and the terms of Senators and Representatives at noon on the 3d day of January, of the years in which such terms would have ended if this article had not been ratified; and the terms of their successors shall then begin.

Section 2. The Congress shall assemble at least once in every year, and such meeting shall begin at noon on the 3d day of January, unless they shall by law appoint a different day.

Section 3. If, at the time fixed for the beginning of the term of the President, the President elect shall have died, the Vice-President elect shall become President. If a President shall not have been chosen before the time fixed for the beginning of his term, or if the President elect shall have failed to qualify, then the Vice-President elect shall act as President until a President shall have qualified; and the Congress may by law provide for the case wherein neither a President elect nor a Vice-President elect shall have qualified, declaring who shall then act as President, or the manner in which one who is to act shall be selected, and such person shall act accordingly until a President or Vice-President shall have qualified.

Section 4. The Congress may by law provide for the case of the death of any of the persons from whom the House of Representatives may choose a President whenever the right of choice shall have devolved upon them, and for the case of the death of any of the persons from whom the Senate may choose a Vice-President whenever the right of choice shall have devolved upon them.

AMENDMENT XXII

No person shall be elected to the office of the President more than twice, and no person who has held the office of President, or acted as President, for more than two years of a term to which some other person was elected President shall be elected to the office of the President more than once. But this article shall not apply to any person holding the office of President when this article was proposed by the Congress, and shall not prevent any person who may be holding the office of President, or acting as President, during the term within which this article becomes operative from holding the office of President or acting as President during the remainder of such term.

Amendment XXV

Section 1.   In case of the removal of the President from office or of his death or resignation, the Vice-President shall become President.

Section 2.   Whenever there is a vacancy in the office of the Vice-President, the President shall nominate a Vice-President who shall take office upon confirmation by a majority vote of both Houses of Congress.

Section 3.   Whenever the President transmits to the President pro tempore of the Senate and the Speaker of the House of Representatives his written declaration that he is unable to discharge the powers and duties of his office, and until he transmits to them a written declaration to the contrary, such powers and duties shall be discharged by the Vice-President as Acting President.

Section. 4.   Whenever the Vice-President and a majority of either the principal officers of the executive departments or of such other body as Congress may by law provide, transmit to the President pro tempore of the Senate and the Speaker of the House of Representatives their written declaration that the President is unable to discharge the powers and duties of his office, the Vice-President shall immediately assume the powers and duties of the office as Acting President.

Thereafter, when the President transmits to the President pro tempore of the Senate and the Speaker of the House of Representatives his written declaration that no inability exists, he shall resume the powers and duties of his office unless the Vice-President and a majority of either the principal officers of the executive department or of such other body as Congress may by law provide, transmit within four days to the President pro tempore of the Senate and the Speaker of the House of Representatives their written declaration that the President is unable to discharge the powers and duties of his office. Thereupon Congress shall decide the issue, assembling within forty-eight hours for that purpose if not in session. If the Congress, within twenty-one days after receipt of the latter written declaration, or, if Congress is not in session, within twenty-one days after Congress is required to assemble, determines by two-thirds vote of both Houses that the President is unable to discharge the powers and duties of his office, the Vice-President shall continue to discharge the same as Acting President, otherwise the President shall resume the powers and duties of his office.

Bibliography

SUGGESTED GENERAL WORKS

Binkley, Wilfred E. *President and Congress*. New York: Knopf, 1947.

Burns, James MacGregor. *Presidential Government*. Boston: Houghton Mifflin, 1966.

Corwin, E. S. *The President, Office and Powers*. 4th ed. New York: New York University Press, 1957.

Hardin, Charles M. *Presidential Power and Accountability*. Chicago: University of Chicago Press, 1974.

Hughes, Emmet John. *The Living Presidency*. New York: Coward, McCann & Geoghegan, 1972.

Hyman, Sidney. *The American Presidency*. New York: Harper, 1954.

Kallenbach, Joseph E. *The American Chief Executive*. New York: Harper & Row, 1966.

Koenig, Louis W. *The Chief Executive*. 3rd ed. New York: Harcourt Brace Jovanovich, 1975.

Laski, Harold. *The American Presidency*. New York: Harper, 1940.

Neustadt, Richard E. *Presidential Power*. New York: Wiley, 1960.

Roche, John P., and Leonard W. Levy, eds. *The Presidency*. New York: Harcourt, Brace & World, 1964.

Rossiter, Clinton. *The American Presidency*. New York: Harcourt, Brace & World, 1964.

Wildavsky, Aaron, ed. *The Presidency*. Boston: Little, Brown, 1969.

CHAPTER ONE

The data on the response to the death of President Kennedy are from a study for the National Opinion Research Center, "The Assassination of

President Kennedy" by Paul B. Sheatsley and Jacob J. Feldman, February, 1964. The great work on the Lincoln myth—some would say a major item in the making of the myth—is Carl Sandburg's monumental life of Lincoln, *Abraham Lincoln, The Prairie Years* (New York: Harcourt, Brace & World, 1926; two volumes) and *Abraham Lincoln, The War Years* (New York: Harcourt, Brace & World, 1939; four volumes). The Lincoln literature is, of course, vast. That on Franklin Roosevelt is now also very large. A biography of particular interest to students of politics is James MacGregor Burns, *Roosevelt: The Lion and the Fox* (New York: Harcourt, Brace & World, 1956). The principal works on John Kennedy are Theodore Sorensen, *Kennedy* (Harper & Row, 1965) and Arthur M. Schlesinger, Jr., *A Thousand Days* (Boston: Houghton Mifflin, 1965). A vivid guide to the character of Harry S Truman is his *Memoirs* (Garden City, N.Y.: Doubleday, 1955–56). On Jackson, there is a complex controversy that can be handled only by wide reading; any simple selection would be tendentious. The views of different presidents on the office have been usefully gathered by Norman J. Small, *Some Presidential Interpretations of the Presidency* (Baltimore: Johns Hopkins, 1930). An interesting argument on the impact of presidential personality is James David Barber, *The Presidential Character* (Englewood Cliffs, N.J.: Prentice-Hall, 1972). The "Caesar" theme is luridly put by Amaury de Riencourt, *The Coming Caesars* (London: Jonathan Cape, 1958). There is more than an echo of this theme in *The Imperial Presidency* by Arthur M. Schlesinger, Jr. (Boston: Houghton Mifflin, 1973). On a closely related topic, see George Reedy, *The Twilight of the Presidency* (New York: Norton, 1970). I have told of confrontation between Kennedy and Blough in *Steel and the Presidency, 1962* (New York: Norton, 1963). Henry Jones Ford's *The Rise and Growth of American Politics* (New York: Meridian, 1963) provided the first reevaluation of the American system after Woodrow Wilson's *Congressional Government* (New York· Macmillan, 1898), a book still worth reading. The literature on the framing of the Constitution is vast, however; see David G. Smith, *The Convention and the Constitution* (New York: St. Martin's, 1965). Perhaps the best subject guide is Chapter 1 of E. S. Corwin's *The President, Office and Powers* (New York: New York University Press, 1957); it is the leading work on the constitutional provisions on the presidency.

CHAPTER TWO
The place of the party system in the political order is gracefully depicted in Pendleton Herring, *The Politics of Democracy* (New York: Norton, 1965). A more severely factual work on parties is Hugh A. Bone, *American Politics and the Party System* (New York: McGraw-Hill, 1966). One of the most useful short works is Aaron B. Wildavsky and Nelson W. Polsby, *Presidential Elections* (New York: Scribner, 1964). The best case

study of a national election campaign remains Theodore H. White, *The Making of the President, 1960* (New York: Atheneum, 1961). For an extended study of conventions, see Paul T. David, Ralph M. Goldman, and Richard ᗡC. Bain, *The Politics of National Party Conventions* (Washington: Brookings, 1960). For data on the phenomena of voting, see Angus Campbell, Philip E. Converse, Warren E. Miller, and Donald E. Stokes, *The American Voter* (New York: Wiley, 1960). Alexander Heard deals with the problem of money in elections in *The Costs of Democracy* (Chapel Hill: University of North Carolina Press, 1960). On the campaign of 1968, see Joe McGinniss, *The Selling of the President, 1968* (New York: Simon & Schuster, 1969).

CHAPTER THREE

Wilfred Binkley's *President and Congress* (New York: Knopf, 1947) remains the most lucid history of the contest between the two branches. One of the more forceful (and pessimistic) discussions is James MacGregor Burns, *The Deadlock of Democracy* (Englewood Cliffs, N.J.: Prentice-Hall, 1963). On the budget, see Aaron B. Wildavsky, *The Politics of the Budgetary Process* (Boston: Little, Brown, 1964). Richard E. Neustadt has traced the rise of systematic presidential review of legislative proposals in "Presidency and Legislation: The Growth of Central Clearance," *American Political Science Review*, XLVIII, no. 3 (September 1954). On the rise of the Council of Economic Advisers, see Edward S. Flash, Jr., *Economic Advice and Presidential Leadership* (New York: Columbia University Press, 1965). For a sympathetic view of Congress today, see Stephen K. Bailey, *The New Congress* (New York: St. Martin's, 1966). Madison's argument on faction is contained in *The Federalist* Number 10.

CHAPTER FOUR

For a discussion of the leading court cases relating to the presidency, see Glendon A. Schubert, Jr., *The Presidency in the Courts* (Minneapolis: University of Minnesota Press, 1957). On the problem of responsibility in the executive branch, see my *Private Power and American Democracy* (New York: Knopf, 1966). An excellent study is Richard Fenno, *The President's Cabinet* (Cambridge, Mass.: Harvard University Press, 1959). The Brownlow Committee's proper title was The President's Committee on Administrative Management; its *Report* was issued in 1937. The working relationship between Franklin Roosevelt and his alter ego has been warmly depicted by Robert E. Sherwood, *Roosevelt and Hopkins* (New York: Harper, 1948). For incisive treatment of the problems of the commissions, see Marver H. Bernstein, *Regulating Business by Independent Commission* (Princeton: Princeton University Press, 1955). A very clear and concise summary of the changes introduced or attempted during the Nixon administration is contained in the second edition of Harold Seidman's *Politics, Position and Power* (New York and London: Oxford University Press, 1975).

CHAPTER FIVE

Virtually every work on the presidency touches on the quality of leadership. Two particularly perceptive studies on this general topic are Richard E. Neustadt, *Presidential Power* (New York: Wiley, 1960) and Pendleton Herring, *Presidential Leadership* (New York: Norton, 1965). The discussion of presidential problems with the steel industry is drawn from my *Steel and the Presidency, 1962* (New York: Norton, 1965) and *The Steel Seizure of 1952* (University: University of Alabama Press, 1960). Regarding some of the difficulties that confronted President Eisenhower, see Emmet John Hughes, *The Ordeal of Power* (New York: Atheneum, 1963). Attention is also called to Theodore Sorensen, *Decision Making in the White House* (New York: Columbia University Press, 1965). The Lowi argument on public support of the president in foreign affairs appears in Theodore J. Lowi, *The Politics of Disorder* (New York: Basic Books, 1971).

CHAPTER SIX

On the changed character of federalism today, see Morton Grodzins, *The American System* (Chicago: Rand McNally, 1966). The Kestenbaum Commission produced one of the best studies of contemporary federalism in its *Report* (Washington, D.C.: Commission on Intergovernmental Relations, 1955). Walter Lippmann's despair of rational public participation in matters relating to foreign affairs is expressed in his *Essays in the Public Philosophy* (Boston: Little, Brown, 1955). A suggestion for change in the presidential system has been made by Herman Finer in *The Presidency: Crisis and Regeneration* (Chicago: University of Chicago Press, 1960). The special relationship between the president and the Court is discussed in Robert Scigliano, *The Supreme Court and the Presidency* (New York: Free Press, 1971).

Index

About the Author

Grant McConnell is Professor of Politics at the University of California, Santa Cruz. He has done graduate study at Oxford University, Harvard University, and the University of California at Berkeley, where he received his Ph.D. Professor McConnell has taught at Mt. Holyoke College, the University of California at Berkeley, and the University of Chicago, and he has held visiting positions at Makerere College (Uganda), Cornell University, and the University of Washington. Among his publications are *Private Power and American Democracy*, *The Decline of Agrarian Democracy*, and *Steel and the Presidency*.